Helping Children Affected by Parental Substance Abuse

D1567927

Helping Children Affected by Parental Substance Abuse

Activities and Photocopiable Worksheets

Tonia Caselman PhD, LCSW

Jessica Kingsley *Publishers*
London and Philadelphia

First published in 2015
by Jessica Kingsley Publishers
73 Collier Street
London N1 9BE, UK
and
400 Market Street, Suite 400
Philadelphia, PA 19106, USA

www.jkp.com

Library of Congress Cataloging in Publication Data
Caselman, Tonia.
  Helping children affected by parental substance abuse : activities and photocopiable worksheets /
Tonia Caselman.
      pages cm
  Includes bibliographical references and index.
  ISBN 978-1-84905-760-8 (alk. paper)
 1. Children of drug abusers–Services for–United States. 2. Children of alcoholics–Services for–United
States. 3. Dysfunctional families–Psychological aspects. 4. Social work with children–United States. I.
Title.
  HV741.C3366 2015
  362.29'130973–dc23
                                    2014046747

British Library Cataloguing in Publication Data
A CIP catalogue record for this book is available from the British Library

ISBN 978 1 84905 760 8
eISBN 978 1 78450 087 0

Printed and bound in Great Britain

Acknowledgments

The author would like to thank Beth Cohen, licensed clinical social worker, for her review of this manuscript and her helpful feedback and suggestions. Besides being a trusted friend, she is a skilled clinician and a creative force who produces inspiration in her employees, colleagues and clients.

Contents

Introduction

Children at Risk

In the US, approximately 8.3 million children under 18 years of age are living with at least one parent who is dependent on illicit drugs or alcohol and in the UK there are approximately 1.2 million children living under the same circumstances (Brisby, Baker and Hedderwick 1997; Cleaver, Unell and Aldgate 2011). This parent might be a custodial parent or a noncustodial parent; it might be a step-parent or an adoptive parent; it might be a parent in a same sex union or in an opposite sex union. Children in these families are at higher risk than children in non-substance-abusing families for a multitude of difficulties including physical problems such as asthma, allergies, headaches, overeating and gastrointestinal disorders (Adger 2004; Felitti *et al.* 1998; Newlin 2011) and behavioral problems such as attempted suicide, depression/anxiety, teenage pregnancy and low self-esteem (Billick, Gotzis and Burgert 1999; El-Guebaly and Offord 1977; Kelley and Fals-Stewart 2004; Russell, Henderson and Blume 1984; Sher 1991). Children of substance-abusing parents also experience a higher incidence of learning disabilities, lower overall academic achievement and higher unemployment as adults (Christofferson and Soothill 2003; Sher 1997). And, finally, children of substance-abusing parents are extremely vulnerable to substance abuse problems themselves (Emshoff and Price 1999; Grant 2000).

In a sample of pediatric psychiatric inpatients, more than 50 percent were found to be children of addicted parents (Rivinus *et al.* 1992). These children also have a greater vulnerability to physical and sexual abuse and neglect; approximately 60 percent of children involved in the child welfare system are children of addicted parents (Backett-Milburn *et al.* 2008; Brook and McDonald 2009).

The Adverse Childhood Experiences Study found that childhood exposure to extreme family dysfunction (including parental substance abuse) is highly associated with health risk behaviors, such as smoking, drinking and overeating, and, consequently, to disease (Felitti *et al.* 1998; Newlin 2011). Lieberman (2000) found that children growing up in these families are vulnerable to economic hardship, medical problems, abuse and neglect.

Children from substance-abusing families themselves describe domestic violence, parent–child relationship problems, parents' "disappearances," concerns about stigma, foreshortened childhoods and early responsibilities for their own, parents' and siblings' needs (Bancroft *et al.* 2004). Unpredictability, disorganization and inconsistency typify the homes where there is an addicted parent (e.g. transient living conditions, inconsistent caregiving, violence, etc.).

Diverse Needs

Children of substance-abusing parents are not a homogeneous group. Research suggests that children's degree of adjustment or maladjustment is the result of an accumulation of risk factors rather than the simple effects of the parental substance abuse alone. Both *general* environmental risk factors (e.g. socioeconomic status, family climate, family health and conflicts, etc.) and *specific* risk factors (e.g. frequency and severity of the substance abuse, the gender of the substance-abusing parent, the substance abuser's behavior while intoxicated or high, the non-substance-abusing parent's level of functioning, the child's level of exposure, the child's interpretation of events, changes in routines, etc.) affect adjustment (Haugland 2003; Werner and Johnson 2004). One study suggested that adult male-to-female aggression in the home had the strongest correlation with children's overall adjustment (Fals-Stewart *et al.* 2003).

Research on children of alcoholics is much more comprehensive than the research on children of drug-abusing parents. While the causes and psychological dynamics appear to be similar between these two groups, one of the major differences is the illegal nature of drug abuse. Children of drug-abusing parents are more likely to lose a parent at an earlier age due to incarceration, violence, illness and overdose. And, while emotional abandonment is common among both groups, a parent's need to seek out illegal drugs can lead to more frequent physical abandonment (Markowitz 2013).

Adjustment

Natural and learned resiliencies, in addition to resources for coping, play an important part in children's adjustment. Close ties to cultural heritage, access to nurturing adults either inside or outside of the family, ability to ask for help, hobbies and extracurricular activities, good problem-solving skills and a curiosity about the world all improve adjustment and coping (Begun and Zweben 1990; Werner and Johnson 2004; Werner and Smith 1989).

Group Format

Because children of substance-abusing parents carry the shame of their family's "secret" they often do not invite friends over or feel that they cannot leave the home in order to socialize. This can cause deficits in social development and, for this reason, group treatment is the treatment modality of choice. Kroll (2004) found that children in substance-abusing families wanted to meet other children in similar circumstances and to talk openly about the problems within the family.

Research recommends a small group format in working with this population (e.g. Moe 1993; Price and Emshoff 2000; Reinert 1999). Small groups can reduce denial, reduce feelings of isolation and shame, create healthy interactions, build trust and present opportunities to try out new solutions to old problems. Learning about substance abuse, sharing personal experiences and learning new social/emotional skills can reduce children's stress, increase their social support systems, change cognitive distortions and provide opportunities for increased self-esteem.

Outcomes for group interventions for children of substance abusers include reduced need to care for parents, reduced beliefs in being able to control the parent's substance abuse, reduced feelings of isolation, increased understanding of their family member's illness, improved school performance and better social relationships (Gregg and Toumbourou 2003; Moe, Johnson and Wade 2008). Outcomes for adolescents also included improved decision making, improved relationships, increased coping strategies, increased resilience and enhanced school performance (Gance-Cleveland 2004).

Group interventions provide information regarding substance abuse, safety, feelings, coping skills, self-care, goal setting, self-esteem and relationship/communication skills. Most groups use a multimodality approach with lectures, discussions, games, worksheets and experiential activities.

Group Cohesion

Research has shown that group cohesion in treatment groups is a significant factor in client outcomes both in inpatient and outpatient settings. This appears to be particularly true with younger populations as they experience the largest positive outcome changes with group cohesion. Cohesion has been found to be strongest when a group lasts more than 12 sessions and includes five to nine members (Burlingame, McClendon and Alonso 2011).

Counselors can facilitate group cohesion by emphasizing member interaction. Important tasks for counselors to practice include finding commonalities between group members, eliciting supportive verbal expressions between members, blocking any aggressive or judgmental expressions between members, and encouraging members to respond empathically to others' emotional expressions. It is also important for children to have fun, as many children of substance-abusing parents are consumed with adult responsibilities and worries. Moe and Pohlman (1989) state, "Play helps not only to connect...but also assists in the healing process" (p.x).

Challenges

There can be several barriers to children's participation in groups: (1) children are unlikely to self-identify, (2) parents may refuse consent due to their own denial or lack of confidence in treatment, and (3) children may be anxious about how they are perceived by peers for attending a group, or (4) they may feel disloyal to their parent by attending. Even after joining a group children may not wish to share right away. Children are very loyal to their parents no matter how problematic that parent's behaviors might be (Harbin 2000).

Prior to beginning a group, children should be provided clear information about participation. This may allay some of their fears and hesitations. It may be helpful to hold discussions about the activities of the group and the children's feelings about attending prior to actually beginning the group (Day, Carey and Surgenor 2006).

Relationship with the Counselor

Trust building is imperative as children of substance-abusing parents often have difficulty trusting others. Counselors should demonstrate consistency, genuine interest, unconditional positive regard and enthusiasm. There is some evidence that the quality of the relationship between counselor and client may be more important to client change than even a particular treatment method (e.g. Shirk and Karver 2003). It should be noted that the therapeutic alliance is not simply a joining task; it is a recurrent task, needing attention throughout treatment. Counselors need to be effective listeners, normalizing feelings and recognizing children's strengths.

Counselors should also be mindful of countertransference as many children of substance-abusing parents can be difficult. Countertransference has been found to affect client outcomes negatively; therefore, managing one's countertransference is important to facilitating positive treatment outcomes (Hayes, Gelso and Hummel 2011).

Moe *et al.* (2008) suggest that the counselor "enter the child's world." This suggests by sitting on the same level as the children, using the children's language and being creative and playful.

Rules

For most children of addicted parents, rules at home change frequently and are inconsistently enforced. Because of this, rules are especially important in group counseling. On the first day, facilitators should begin by asking the group why rules are important. Once everyone has shared, a summary of the children's reasons should be given, stressing that the main reason for rules is so everyone can remain safe and have a good time. In establishing the rules for the group, be sure to create rules that describe what children are TO DO instead of what they are NOT to do. For example:

Instead of…	Use…
Don't interrupt	One person talks at a time
Don't share outside what others have said	What we say here, stays here
No put-downs	Only positive respsonses to others

Ask children why each specific rule is important. Then make sure that group rules are posted in full view of everyone and reviewed at each group session. Try not to make too many rules. A suggested number is five rules.

Rules also need clearly understood consequences if broken. Again, it is important to be clear and consistent. Let children know ahead of time what the consequences will be. For example, first offense: a warning; second offense: a five-minute time-out; third offense: longer time-out or leave the group. However, each group session should give children a clean slate. Facilitators should treat children like they are capable of following the rules.

Important Tips for Facilitators

- Be clear about issues of confidentiality and duty to report, so that children know what will happen to information they give.

- Do not criticize the child's alcohol or drug-using parent. Children love their parents and are loyal to them even under difficult situations.

- Allow children to have a choice whether or not they wish to take home worksheets or art projects from the group.

- Give permission to talk but also permission *not* to say anything. Mistrust and suspicion of "outsiders" are often issues for children of substance-abusing parents. Be patient and allow children to engage in their own time.

- If a child becomes emotionally dysregulated during any of the activites, be sure to remain calm and nonjudgmental. If the activity is too stressful for the child, allow her/him to discontinue it and encourage her/him to practice familiar coping skills.

- Use direct and clear language (straight talk) when discussing substance abuse, thereby overcoming the barrier that the topic is taboo or too terrible to talk about.

- Caution children not to confront parents about drinking or using unless under the guidance/protection of another adult. Emphasize to them that it is not safe.

- Be sensitive to cultural differences. If the child is from a different culture, learn about that culture, including family structure, customs, beliefs and values. This knowledge will be valuable in effectively helping the child.

- Be careful about self-disclosure. Keep clear boundaries. Too much self-disclosure on the part of the counselor can replicate substance-abusing family dynamics.

- Do not make plans that you cannot keep. Stability and consistency in relationships are necessary if children are to develop trust.

- Be current in the knowledge of community resources. Help children and their parents make links to needed programs and services.

- Be flexible, playful and have a good sense of humor!

- Finally, facilitators should use their best judgement in selecting activities and worksheets in this book. Not every suggestion will be relevant for every group.

Reporting Suspected Abuse

All states and countries have legislation regarding mandatory reporting of suspected child abuse and neglect. Counselors should familiarize themselves with this and also follow agency policies for reporting suspected abuse or neglect. Children should be told that counselors must share this type of information and cannot keep this confidential.

If a child discloses or if the counselor observes that the child is injured, the counselor should meet with her/him one-on-one after the group session, gather information about what happened and then if a report is warranted, let her/him know that you will have to report to Child Protective Services.

This Book

Helping Children Affected by Parental Substance Abuse is designed to assist counselors, social workers, psychologists and teachers in facilitating educational/treatment groups for children of addicted parents. Given the large number of children in substance-abusing homes, the degree of pain they suffer in childhood and the lifetime consequences for many of them in adulthood, *Helping Children Affected by Parental Substance Abuse* can help children overcome shame, let go of a need for control and develop coping skills, support networks and resiliency.

Helping Children Affected by Parental Substance Abuse provides group facilitators with step-by-step instructions for leading a group. It covers nine content areas that address pertinent topics for children of substance-abusing parents. Each chapter reviews the research literature, presents scripts for facilitators to read or paraphrase with the children, offers discussion questions/activities and includes worksheets, making it easy for group facilitators simply to pick up the book and lead a group with minimal preparation. Activities and worksheets do not need to be done in any particular order so facilitators should use their own discretion based on the needs of their particular groups. In addition, an entire chapter's content does not have to be completed in a single session. Facilitators can use multiple sessions to cover content from any chapter. Appendix F has additional activities if facilitators wish to extend a particular chapter's content. All pages marked with a star are photocopiable.

CHAPTER 1
Understanding Addiction

Introduction

Research with adults of alcoholics found that adults who grew up in substance-abusing homes remembered feeling like their families were not "normal" but not understanding why (Backett-Milburn *et al.* 2008). They doubted their own perceptions. They were taught to deny the existence of the problems and their own feelings about it.

Children become aware of their parents' substance abuse patterns at a very early age. However, growing up with addiction in the home has been compared to having an elephant in the living room. Everyone knows it's there but no one mentions it. Children witness their parents' substance abuse while simultaneously hearing parents refuting it. For example, if Dad is passed out on the couch smelling of alcohol, Mom may insist that he is exhausted from work. Or if Mom becomes enraged and violent while high, she may insist that the children see her as tender and loving. Children observe changes in their parents' personalities and become confused regarding which personality is the "real" parent. They may also blame themselves for their parents' sudden changes in mood, not realizing that drugs or alcohol are the culprit. They learn to doubt their own perceptions.

Research has identified the "Don't talk" and "Don't feel" rules within substance-abusing families (Ruben 2001). To be a good child in a substance-abusing family, one has to deny the substance abuse and other family problems (Ackerman 1989). If children are not educated about substance abuse, they remain confused and blame themselves. Many children of substance-abusing parents lack basic information about alcohol and drugs and the disease concept of chemical dependency.

Best Practices and Treatment Recommendations

Most programs for children of substance-abusing parents provide clear information about drugs/alcohol and addiction in order to help correct children's false perceptions (Cuijpers 2005). Children attach meaning to their parents' behaviors but, because of their limited knowledge and life experiences, the meaning they

15

make is often mistaken and full of self-blame. Children need an accurate framework for what they are experiencing. Indeed, studies show that understanding addiction helps children overcome misplaced self-blame and guilt about parental substance abuse (Price and Emshoff 1997).

Indeed, psychoeducation is one of the most effective evidence-based practices for many kinds of illnesses (Lukens and McFarlane 2004). For children of substance abusers, research has shown that insight is a significant contributor to resilience (Wolin and Wolin 1996). Adolescents, in a support group for children of addicted parents, identified increased knowledge concerning addiction as one of the main benefits of participation (Gance-Cleveland 2004).

Moe *et al.* (2008) describe the importance of education in helping children to separate their loved ones from the disease of addiction. The leaders in substance abuse treatment use education about drugs and alcohol in their children's programs. For example, Substance Abuse and Mental Health Services Administration (SAMHSA) uses education in its Children's Program Kit and the Betty Ford program covers the disease of alcoholism and other drug addictions during the very first day of its children's program.

In order to assess children's feelings about their parents' substance abuse problems, the following questions can be used:

- Do you worry about your mom or dad's drinking/using drugs?

- Do you sometimes feel that you are the reason your parent drinks/uses drugs so much?

- Are you ashamed to have your friends come to your house, and are you finding more and more excuses to stay away from home?

- Do you sometimes feel that you hate your parents when they are drinking/using drugs, and then feel guilty for hating them?

- Have you been watching how much your parent drinks/uses drugs?

- Do you try to make your parents happy so they won't get upset and drink/use drugs more?

- Do you feel you can't talk about drinking/using drugs in your home—or even how you feel inside?

- Do you sometimes drink or take drugs to forget about things that you feel inside?

- Do you feel if your parents really loved you, they wouldn't drink/use drugs so much?

- Do you want to start feeling better?

(Brooks 1981)

Getting Started

It is essential to establish an atmosphere of safety and trust—the group should be a place where children can talk and ask and feel. The physical and emotional environment should be warm, accepting and playful with rules that are predictable and consistent (see the Introduction for suggestions about establishing rules). Included in the rules should be a statement about confidentiality. Be sure also to go over the limitations of confidentiality as it pertains to mandatory reporting of child abuse/neglect.

Begin the first session with an ice breaker so that children can get to know one another. Any age-appropriate ice breaker is fine but here are a few ideas:

- **Pass the Toilet Paper:** Hold up a roll of toilet paper. Announce to the group that it is indeed a roll of toilet paper and that you will be passing it around for everyone to take as much as they need "to get the job done." Do not explain what "the job" is—simply let the group think what they will. Take some for yourself and pass it around the room. After everyone has taken what they need, explain that each person will say one thing about themselves for every square of toilet paper that they pulled off from the roll.

- **Ice Breaker Bingo:** Prior to the group, facilitators will need to create Bingo cards with 25 squares that describe various child preferences and activities. (These can include things like "I love to swim," "I hate brussels sprouts," "My favorite meal is breakfast," "I like being outside," "I have a pet," "I use my nickname instead of my given name," "My favorite sport is football," "I've moved in the last six months," "My favorite color is pink," etc.) Each child receives a Bingo card and a pen or pencil. The goal is to be the first person to get signatures on five squares in a row (horizontally, vertically or diagonally). To collect a signature, another group member must truthfully answer "yes" to the statement in that square. A child can only sign *one* square on another child's Bingo card.

- **A Mighty Wind Blows:** Arrange chairs in a circle facing the center. Instruct children to take a seat. The facilitator will call out, "A mighty wind blows for everyone who (*fill in the blank*)" and everyone who is affected must stand up and quickly find another chair. The first one to find a new seat calls out proudly, "And my name is (*name of child*)!" Repeat over and over again until most children have been able to announce their names. If anyone is missed, be sure to have her/him announce her/his name at the end of the game. Some ideas for what makes a "mighty wind blow" include those who have a younger brother, have an older sister, have a dog, have a cat, like vanilla ice cream more than chocolate, like peanut butter, like math, like video games, ate cereal for breakfast this morning, etc.

The overall goals of meeting with children of substance abusers should be to help them feel freed from guilt and shame around their parents' substance use, to gain a sense of support, to have hope and to allow themselves joy and fun. Important points that should be reiterated over and over are:

- Everybody gets hurt in a substance-abusing family.

- Children whose parents drink or use drugs too much are not alone.

- Children can't cause, control or cure a parent's substance abuse.

- There are many good ways for kids to take care of themselves.

- It is healing to identify and express feelings.

- It is OK to talk about parental drinking or using to a special group or a friend.

- It is important for children to identify and use a trusted support system outside of the family.

- There are many ways of problem solving and coping with parental substance abuse.

(Dies and Burghardt 1991; Nastasi and DeZolt 1994)

General Suggestions

- Clarify and validate children's stories about their experiences with substance-abusing parents.

- Emphasize over and over again that addiction is a disease and children do not cause it.

- Provide lots of emotional support while explaining addiction.

- Reassure children that they are not alone in their experiences; point to the other group members.

- Maintain a small library of books, pamphlets and articles that have been written for children regarding parental substance abuse.

- Instill hope. Explain that addicted parents can and often do get better but, even if they don't, children can still get help for themselves.

- Children may have lots of questions regarding addiction and recovery. Always answer these questions honestly and in a developmentally appropriate manner. While not exhaustive, here are some responses that may be helpful:

  ○ If asked about parents' "lying," explain that it is a part of the disease called *denial.*

  ○ If asked about recovery, explain that recovery is a process of managing the disease of substance abuse; it happens most commonly when people go to treatment; it takes a long time and it often includes relapses.

  ○ If asked about relapse, explain that it is like when you've newly learned to ride a bicycle: you can be riding fine for a while and then fall unexpectedly. Relapse is when a substance-abusing person is in recovery (not using) and then uses again for a period; it is to be expected.

  ○ If parents are in recovery and moody, explain that it is normal for recovery to start with feelings of anxiety, restlessness and irritability.

Script

"An addiction is a disease that makes a person think about drugs or alcohol most of the time and damages her/his ability to control or stop drinking/using. People with addiction need to drink or use drugs kind of like when you need to sneeze—you feel that tickle in your nose and just have to sneeze. The person is stuck on the drug or alcohol. It's not their fault. They are good people with a disease.

Drinking too much alcohol and taking certain kinds of drugs can change the way a person acts. If a parent drinks too much alcohol or takes drugs not recommended by a doctor, it can be embarrassing for the kids. In fact, some kids won't have friends over because they are worried about what might happen if their parent drinks too much or gets high. Some kids think it's their fault but it's not.

If your mom or dad has problems with drugs or alcohol, there are some things that you should know:

- Your parent is not a bad person. She/he has an illness that makes her/him 'glued' to drugs or alcohol.

- Children have nothing to do with this illness. It's not your fault.

- Your parent may not be ready to get well yet. Or your parent may have tried to get well but went back to drinking or drugs. That is to be expected. It's called *relapse*.

- You cannot make your parent quit drinking or getting high. It's not your job.

- You are not alone. There are lots of other kids whose parents have drug and alcohol problems.

- There are good ways for children to take care of themselves.

We will talk lots more about all of this over the next few weeks. Always feel free to ask any questions and tell the group anything that is bothering you."

Activities

(1) DRUGS, DRUGS, DRUGS

OBJECTIVE

To increase understanding of drugs' effects.

MATERIALS

Dry erase board or flip chart and markers.

DIRECTIONS

Write a list of drugs on a dry erase board or flip chart (examples: aspirin, wine, beer, penicillin, marijuana, Xanax, insulin, Valium, heroin, etc.). Ask the children which drugs can change how a person *acts*. Explain that people who use too much or too many of these drugs become "drunk" or "high." Then ask them to name ways that people act when they drink too much alcohol or get high (examples: fall asleep, yell, fall, forget things, say stupid things, etc.). Write these on the dry erase board/flip chart. Explain that people who use these substances so much that it causes them problems at home or at work have a disease called "addiction."

FOLLOW-UP DISCUSSION QUESTIONS

- Which of the listed drunk or high behaviors have you seen?

- Which drug names did you recognize?

- What kind of problems do the listed behaviors cause (at home, at work, in relationships, etc.)?

- How does learning this information help you to be less confused?

(2) ADDICTION IS A STUCK-ON DISEASE

OBJECTIVE
To increase understanding of addiction.

MATERIALS
Construction paper and glue.

DIRECTIONS
Explain to the group that people who drink too much alcohol or use too many mood-changing drugs often have problems at work, at home and in their relationships. When this happens we say that they have an *addiction*. This doesn't make them bad people; it simply means they have a sickness called addiction. An addiction is craving, needing and being "stuck on" drugs or alcohol.

Instruct children to take two pieces of construction paper and glue them together. When the glue has dried, ask them to try to separate the two papers. (This will often end up with children tearing the paper. Don't allow them to become frustrated with this task. The idea is that it is impossible.)

FOLLOW-UP DISCUSSION QUESTIONS

- Was it possible to pull apart the papers?

- How did you feel while trying to separate them?

- Did you use bad sheets of paper when you glued them?

- Do you think that your parent is a bad person for using drugs or alcohol?

(3) HOW MUCH DO YOU KNOW GAME

OBJECTIVE
To enhance understanding of alcoholism and drug addiction.

MATERIALS
Appendix A and paper or pen for scoring.

DIRECTIONS
Inform the group that it is important to understand some things about alcohol and drug abuse. Explain that you will be reading questions one by one about drugs and alcohol (see Appendix A). If they think they know the answer to the question, they should quickly slap the table (ringers, whistles, etc. can also be used). The first person to slap the table gets an opportunity to answer the question. If she/he answers correctly she/he earns a point. Incorrect answers are not penalized. The person with the most points wins.

FOLLOW-UP DISCUSSION QUESTIONS

- What new things did you learn in this game?
- What information surprised you?
- How does learning this information change how you feel?
- What questions do you have after playing this game?

(4) COVERED UP

OBJECTIVE
To increase understanding that a loved one is separate from the addiction.

MATERIALS
Paper bags, paper, scissors and crayons or markers.

DIRECTIONS
Remind the group that their parents love them and are good people—they just have a disease called addiction. Direct them to cut out and color a figure that represents their parent (similar to a single paper doll—these can be drawn on paper prior to the group). Then have them color a paper bag to represent addiction. On the bottom of the bag help the children cut out two holes where the legs of the paper dolls can fit through. Then help the children place their paper "parent" inside the paper bag, fitting their legs through the holes in the bottom. If they wish, children can play with these parent paper dolls.

FOLLOW-UP DISCUSSION QUESTIONS

- Even though your parent paper doll can walk around OK, what problems might she/he have being inside the sack (addiction)?

- When other people look at your parent paper doll, do they see the person or the "addiction" (paper sack)?

- How could you see the "person" rather than the "addiction?"

- What did you learn from this activity?

(5) THE 7 CS

OBJECTIVE
To reinforce the National Association for Children of Alcoholics "7 Cs of Addiction."

MATERIALS
Dry erase board or flip chart and markers.

DIRECTIONS
The National Association for Children of Alcoholics suggests that children dealing with family addiction learn and use the "7 Cs of Addiction" which are:

I didn't	**Cause** it.
I can't	**Cure** it.
I can't	**Control** it.
I can	**Care** for myself.
By	**Communicating** my feelings,
Making healthy	**Choices**, and
By	**Celebrating** myself.

Write the 7 Cs on a dry erase board or flip chart. Then have children break up into small groups of two or three and instruct them to create a rap or song using the 7 Cs. When everyone has completed their song or rap, invite them to perform it for the group.

OPTIONAL: The performances can be audio taped or video taped in order to be played back at a later time.

FOLLOW-UP DISCUSSION QUESTIONS

- What did it feel like to sing or rap the 7 Cs?

- Do you think you'll be able to remember your song or rap to use during stressful times?

- What would you like to do with your song or rap now that it's created?

- Of the 7 Cs, which one will be easiest for you to remember and practice? Which one might be the hardest for you to remember and practice?

Worksheet Discussion Questions

Survey has a list of ten questions about typical feelings and behaviors children of substance-abusing parents have reported. Children answer "yes" or "no" to each item. After completing the worksheet, the following discussion questions can be used:

- How many questions did you answer "yes" to?

- Were you surprised at how many "yes"s you had?

- What are your thoughts about the questions?

- Of all ten questions, which one do you think you do the most?

Word Search has 12 words hidden that have to do with parental alcohol or drug problems. Children simply find and circle the words: addiction, alcohol, denial, disease, drugs, family, hangover, hooked, parent, problems, relapse and stuck. After completing the word search, the following discussion questions can be used:

- Do you know what each of the words in the word search means? Do you have any questions about any of the words?

- Where have you heard some of the words before?

- Are there other words that you have heard regarding drugs or alcohol but don't know what they mean?

- Which of these words is hardest for you to say?

Stuck explains that addiction means a person is stuck on drugs or alcohol. It asks children to draw two pictures of other things that can get stuck (like a magnet on metal). If children have a difficult time identifying items that get stuck, some ideas include gum in hair, cockleburs on socks, cat hair on clothing, etc. After drawing the pictures, the following discussion questions can be used:

- What does *stuck* actually mean?

- Have you ever had anything stuck?

- How hard is it for the things you drew to get unstuck without someone helping?

- How hard do you think it might be for your parent to get unstuck from drugs or alcohol?

Addiction Hurts asks children to list ways that addiction has hurt both their parent and them. If children have a difficult time naming ways that addiction has hurt, give them prompts in various domains such as relationships, self-esteem, work/school, hobbies, etc. After completing the worksheet, the following discussion questions can be used:

- How difficult was it to come up with ways that addiction hurts? Was it difficult because it was hard to think of things or was it difficult because it was painful?

- When you look over your list, what are your thoughts and feelings?

- Who else in your family has addiction hurt?

- Who in your family do you think is most worried about addiction hurting your family members?

Dear Addiction suggests that children think of addiction as something distinct from their parents—a separate entity, if you will. Using sentence prompts, it asks them to write a letter to addiction stating how it has hurt their family, how they can't control it, how they refuse to keep its secrets and who they can talk to. After completing the letter, the following discussion questions can be used:

- How do you feel after writing this letter?

- The letter said that you can't control addiction. Have you ever tried to? How? How hard will it be to give up trying to control it?

- Besides the person you mentioned in the letter, who else can you talk to when you are feeling worried or upset about your parent's drinking or drug abuse?

- What would you like to do with your letter now?

Survey

Kids who have a parent with a drug or alcohol problem have described many feelings and behaviors that are a direct result of their parents' disease. Some of them are listed below. Circle YES or NO to each question based on whether or not it is true for you.

Do you worry about your parent's drinking or drug use?   YES   NO

Are you embarrassed to invite your friends over because of your parent's drinking or drug use?   YES   NO

Do you ever feel really angry with your parent for her/his drinking or drug abuse?   YES   NO

Do you ever try to please your parent so that she/he won't drink or use drugs?   YES   NO

Do you ever lie about or make excuses for your parent's behavior on drugs or alcohol?   YES   NO

Do you ever feel like it's your fault that your parent uses drugs and/or alcohol?   YES   NO

Do you ever try to hide your parent's drugs and/or alcohol?   YES   NO

Do you ever argue with your parent or with other people about your parent's drinking or drug abuse?   YES   NO

Do you ever feel afraid to talk about your parent's drugs and/or alcohol?   YES   NO

Do you ever feel like your home is "not normal?"   YES   NO

Word Search

Find the following words:

addiction   hangover
alcohol   hooked
denial   parent
disease   problems
drugs   relapse
family   stuck

R S A Y P R O B L E M S

E F L W X P M Q F E K G

L K C T J A W L X I F A

A A O H D R U G S A A E

P D H A C E Y H D S M H

S D O N R N W D V D I L

E I L G E T I Z I O L H

S C C O A C B S K I Y S

I T Q V H O O K E D T T

D I S E A S E E W G E U

R O O R S O D V J B I C

T N O E D E N I A L R K

Stuck

Addiction is being stuck to something like drugs or alcohol. Can you think of other things that get stuck? Draw two pictures of things that get stuck (example: magnets on metal).

Addiction Hurts

Addiction hurts the person it's stuck to and it hurts that person's loved ones. How has addiction hurt your parent? How has it hurt you? Make two lists below.

How Addiction Hurts My Parent

How Addiction Hurts Me

Dear Addiction

If your parent's addiction was something that you could talk to or write to, what would you like to tell it? Fill in the blanks in the letter below and then add anything else that you would like to say to addiction.

Dear Addiction,

I don't like the way that you _____

_____. You've hurt my _____

by_____

_____

You've hurt me by_____

_____.

I can't make you leave but I can make sure that you don't make me feel _____

_____ any more!

In fact, I'm not going to keep your stupid secrets any more.

I'm going to talk to _____

whenever I want. You don't have any power over me any more._____

_____

_____

Signed,

_____

CHAPTER 2
Letting Go of Shame

Introduction

Shame strongly affects children of substance-abusing parents (Hadley, Holloway and Mallinckrodt 1993). Research suggests that, unlike guilt, shame results in anger and interpersonal hostility either towards the self or others (Tangney and Dearing 2002). Chronic internalized shame has also been associated with mental health problems and substance abuse disorders (Andrews and Hunter 1997; Luoma *et al.* 2008).

It is important to distinguish shame from guilt. Shame is a global, painful distress about one's self, whereas guilt is a specific negative feeling about something that one has done (Wiechelt 2007). Where guilt increases responsibility and moves people to action (such as making amends), shame is immobilizing and causes withdrawal and isolation (Potter-Efron 2002). Guilt says, "I did something wrong"; shame says, "I'm a terrible person."

Shame produces harmful secrets and damages self-esteem. Shame tells the child she/he is unlovable and inadequate, creating a desire to hide or disappear (Lewis 1992). Shame activates anger, depression, anxiety and overstated pride. When parents are unable to provide stable, nurturing environments, children develop mistrust, insecurities and shame. Indeed, empirical research has shown that poor family cohesion (as is so often the case in substance-abusing families) is associated with children's deep-seated shame (Hadley *et al.* 1993).

Adults who reflected on childhoods in substance-abusing families reported feeling tremendous shame because their families were so different from other families (Hadley *et al.* 1993). A common theme in children's descriptions of home life with addicted parents is embarrassment and attempts to hide parental substance abuse from others (Backett-Milburn *et al.* 2008; Bancroft *et al.* 2004; Barnard and Barlow 2003). Children feel shame when a parent is brought home by the police for public drunkenness or is incarcerated; they feel shame when they have to assist the staggering, unruly parent in front of other people; they feel shame when they cannot have friends to the home because of what they might see. Children love their parents so they often justify the parent's behavior and blame themselves.

Children become part of a "conspiracy of silence" where shame and the fear of consequences isolate them from potential sources of support. Children of drug-abusing parents, in particular, are part of a subculture in which secrecy is necessary due to possible police raids, imprisonment and the consequences of criminal activity (Hogan and Higgins 2001).

Best Practices and Treatment Recommendations

First and foremost, an empathic and respectful therapeutic relationship can help children overcome feelings of shame. Active listening, reflecting and open communication increase feelings of validation and self-acceptance (Deblinger and Runyon 2005). And, because children are hypersensitive to adult responses, counselors should be careful not to exhibit behaviors which may appear critical or disapproving when children share stories of their parents' substance abuse. Subtle behaviors such as raised eyebrows, looking away, interrupting or laughing can be perceived as shaming. Counselors should reflect back children's stories in a normal tone of voice even if children share them in a quieter or shameful manner. Creating an accepting and safe environment helps children to share their stories and to reveal cognitive distortions associated with their experiences (Deblinger and Runyon 2005).

Second, the antithesis of shame is disclosure. By repeatedly discussing and/or writing about distressing experiences, children can reduce feelings of shame (Deblinger and Runyon 2005). Research with depressed adults found that facilitating disclosure of shameful symptoms and behaviors improved treatment outcomes (Hook and Andrews 2005). And brain research found that trauma survivors without post-traumatic sress disorder (PTSD) symptoms activate verbal areas of the brain when remembering aspects of their trauma (Lanius *et al.* 2004).

Identifying, challenging and changing cognitive distortions which underlie feelings of shame can help decrease psychological distress associated with shame (Feiring, Taska and Lewis 1998). Children filled with shame have flawed and inaccurate thinking. Challenging and replacing these thinking errors with more rational thoughts can reduce shame. Because of shame's heightened self-consciousness, Parker and Thomas (2009) also recommend that treatment focus on building awareness of how the self is different from actions or cognitions.

And, finally, there is limited but increasing research data regarding compassion-focused therapy for the treatment of shame and self-criticism (Gilbert and Procter 2006; Mayhew and Gilbert 2008). In compassion-focused therapy clients develop an internal compassionate relationship with themselves by distinguishing self-criticism and self-compassion thoughts, and engaging in compassionate behavior towards themselves (Gilbert 2009).

General Suggestions

- Create trusting relationships with each child—a positive relationship shows children that they are worthwhile.

- Reiterate over and over again that it is not the children's fault that a parent drinks or uses drugs.

- Help children identify, challenge and change cognitive distortions regarding shame and blame.

- Encourage children to have good posture and to look people in the eye. This counters the "shrinking away" tendency that shame produces.

- Assess whether or not children are being bullied at school or in their neighborhoods and help parents and teachers take action to eliminate it.

- Help children talk out their stories of trauma and shame.

- Remind children to be kind and compassionate with themselves, teaching them to be tolerant of their mistakes and failures.

Script

"Think of the most embarrassing experience of your life. Or a time when you were totally humiliated. Doesn't it feel awful? Shame is like that—it's that really deep painful feeling caused by intense embarrassment and humiliation. It makes you feel very self-conscious and unlovable.

Lots of times kids whose parents use drugs and alcohol feel shame but this kind of shame is a lie. It's not your fault that your parent uses drugs or alcohol; a parent's mistakes are not your mistakes. You are not responsible for the problem and you are not responsible for fixing it.

We are going to work on letting go of any shame that you might have about your parent's drug or alcohol problem. No, you're not perfect and yes, you've made your own mistakes but, hey, EVERYONE makes mistakes. We want you to accept yourself, warts and all. So, repeat after me:

- I didn't cause my parent's substance abuse.
    (*Wait for children to repeat.*)

- I can't heal my parent's substance abuse.
    (*Wait for children to repeat.*)

- I can't control or manage my parent's substance abuse.
    (*Wait for children to repeat.*)

- But I can take care of and control myself.
    (*Wait for children to repeat.*)"

Activities

(1) BAG OF SHAME

OBJECTIVE
To identify the negative effects of shame and the benefits of getting rid of it.

MATERIALS
Paper, pens, tape, a backpack or satchel and bricks.

DIRECTIONS
Explain to the group that carrying around shame is a huge weight to bear. Direct them to write down some of their shameful thoughts and feelings on a piece of paper and then fold this paper around a brick and tape it on. Have them put these covered bricks into a backpack or satchel. Ask one of the children to wear or carry it while walking around the room for several minutes. When enough time has elapsed so the child appears tired of the weight, ask her/him to stop. Then direct the child to unload the backpack, making statements such as "I don't need this shame," "Shame is a heavy burden to bear," "I'm getting rid of this shame," etc. Ask the child to wear or carry the empty backpack or satchel for a few minutes. Have several of the children in the group repeat this exercise or, if there are enough materials, have everyone in the group do the exercise at the same time.

FOLLOW-UP DISCUSSION QUESTIONS
- How was the experience different carrying the heavy load versus carrying the lighter load?
- How did it feel to get rid of the weight?
- How do you think you would feel "lighter" if you unloaded your shame? How would your life be different?
- What are some of the specific shaming thoughts that you need to get rid of?

(2) LETTING GO

OBJECTIVE
To externalize and release shame.

MATERIALS
None.

DIRECTIONS

Explain to the group that you will be doing an imaginative exercise with them. Tell them to get into a relaxed position and, if they would like, to close their eyes. (If a child is uncomfortable closing her/his eyes, she/he may keep them open.) Explain that you will be reading to them and that you would like them to imagine the pictures in their minds. Then read the following:

> *Imagine yourself sitting next to a beautiful river on a warm, sunny day. You feel safe, confident and strong as you watch the water moving along gently. Imagine that there is a caring person sitting next to you. Perhaps this person is someone you know personally, perhaps it is a person you have read about, perhaps it is someone that you would like to make up in your imagination. But know that this person is wise and honest and kind. Do you have that person in mind? Good.*

> *Now imagine a small, empty, open box just in front of you. Continue feeling safe, confident and strong as you bring to mind something you are ashamed of regarding your parent's drinking or drug abuse. Don't let it feel difficult. Just remember it gently. Feel the support of the caring person sitting next to you as you remember it. Imagine it lying on the ground in front of you near the empty box. It's also small. In fact, it will fit nicely into the box. Do you see it? Accept it and then pick it up and put it in the box. Now put a lid on the box. Make sure that the lid fits securely. Pick up the box and carefully walk it over to the river where you gently put it into the water and watch it being taken downstream. Say good-bye to it as it floats off into the distance. Let yourself feel relief…freed…peace. Watch it float away until you can no longer see it.*

FOLLOW-UP DISCUSSION QUESTIONS

- Could you imagine your shame floating away? How did that feel?
- Who was the caring person sitting next to you? Did it help having her/him there?
- What do you think that caring person would have said to you for letting go of your shame?
- How could you use this exercise on your own (by yourself) when you are feeling shame about something related to your parent's drinking or drug abuse?

(3) ACTING OPPOSITE

OBJECTIVE

To reduce shame surrounding difficult feelings and receive support from others.

MATERIALS

None.

DIRECTIONS

Explain to the group that one way to lessen a feeling's grip on us is to act *opposite* to the way we act when we feel that feeling. For example, when we feel fear, we often move away from the thing that we fear. The opposite of this would be to approach the fear-producing event. Explain that shame often causes people to keep difficult feelings to themselves, so, in order to act in the *opposite* way that we act when we feel shame, it is important to *talk* about it.

Ask the group to think about something that they feel shame about (e.g. a parent's drinking, a sibling's unplanned pregnancy, conflict in the home, etc.). After everyone acknowledges that they have a shame event/situation in mind, ask group members to share their shame event/situation one at a time. Remind everyone that this information is confidential and should not leave the group. (If some children do not wish to share, do not force them.) After each admission of a shameful event/situation, instruct the group to say to the person, "Thank you for trusting us with that information. You have a lot of courage."

FOLLOW-UP DISCUSSION QUESTIONS

- How difficult was it for you to share your feelings? What feelings did you have sharing something that you do not usually share with others?

- How did you feel hearing others sharing something that *they* do not usually share?

- Do you need to talk more about what you shared?

- What kind of support would you like from the group right now?

(4) TURN IT OFF

OBJECTIVE

To create a sense of control over shameful memories.

MATERIALS

None.

DIRECTIONS

Explain that while people cannot change things that have happened to them, they can refuse to let those memories control them. Explain that in this exercise they will be using their imaginations to take control over a shameful memory. Ask the group members to imagine a large TV screen in front of them and to imagine a shameful memory being played on it. Wait a few seconds to make sure that everyone has selected a memory to play on their "TV screen." Then ask them to imagine having the remote control in their hands. Tell them first to imagine turning the volume down. Wait a few seconds and then tell them to imagine turning the sound completely off. Wait a few more seconds and then tell them to imagine changing the channel or turning the TV off. Afterwards tell the group that they can use this technique whenever they have a memory that they want to take control of.

FOLLOW-UP DISCUSSION QUESTIONS

- What was it like to have your memory placed on a TV screen rather than inside your own head?
- What was it like having the remote control to your memories?
- Was it easier to turn down the volume, change the channel or turn the TV off?
- Do you think you could use this technique again? Would you do it with other memories as well?
- Do you have any questions?

(5) TWO SIDES OF A BRAIN

OBJECTIVE
To identify and change cognitive distortions.

MATERIALS
A piece of gray construction paper, a piece of pink construction paper, markers and tape.

DIRECTIONS
Prior to the group, draw pictures of brains on the two pieces of construction paper. Explain that these represent positive thoughts and negative thoughts. Ask for three volunteers to come forward; tape one "brain" to one child's forehead and tape the other "brain" to another child's forehead; instruct the third child to stand between them. Introduce the rest of the group to the child in the middle and the two sides of her/his "brain." Then ask the middle child to talk about a mistake she/he has made (e.g. yelled at a sibling, did poorly on homework, hid the vegetables that she/he didn't want to eat, etc.). Direct the child with the gray brain to make a couple of accusations about the child based on this information ("You're a mean person!" "You're stupid!" "You're dishonest!" etc.). Stop this after a few seconds and ask the middle child how she/he feels listening to that side of her/his "brain." Then direct her/him to turn her/his back on that "stinkin' thinkin'" and listen to the other side of his "brain." Have that child respond with more accurate and reasonable statements such as "We all get frustrated with our siblings. You may have yelled at your sister/brother but if anyone else tried to hurt her/him, I know you'd defend her/him!" or "Everyone does poorly on their schoolwork at some time or another. You're a smart kid. You'll do better!" or "Oh, my gosh, that's hilarious that you gave your dog your vegetables! Maybe I'll try that!" Then ask the middle child how she/he feels listening to that side of her/his "brain." Allow additional children to participate.

FOLLOW-UP DISCUSSION QUESTIONS

- How hard was it for those of you who had to admit a mistake? Do you think it takes courage to admit mistakes?

- Which kind of thinking makes you feel better?

- What do you think happens if you constantly listen to the negative thoughts?

- Which side of the brain was the more honest side? What can you do to listen to that side more often?

Worksheet Discussion Questions

Recognizing Shame helps children identify the feeling of shame by asking questions and directing them to imagine what shame feels like through their various senses. After completing the worksheet, the following discussion questions can be used:

- Where do you feel shame in your body? What does it feel like there?

- On a scale of 1–10 (1 being the lowest and 10 being the highest), how much do you hate feeling shame? How long have you recognized the feeling?

- What are the things that trigger your feelings of shame?

- How hopeful are you that you can get rid of your feelings of shame (because there IS hope!)?

How Shame Affects Me lists various ways in which shame can be experienced. It asks children to check the items that apply to them and to rate those items according to their strength/influence in their lives. After completing the worksheet, the following discussion questions can be used:

- How many of the items did you mark on the worksheet? Which items do you NOT have trouble with?

- Which one of the items that you marked with an X has the highest number (i.e. affects you the most)? How long have you been struggling with this?

- What can you do to make this better? How can other people help you?

- Did anything surprise you while completing this worksheet? What was it?

Finding Coping Skills lists different triggers and byproducts of shame and asks children to search the page to find a coping skill for each one. After completing the worksheet, the following discussion questions can be used:

- Which coping skill did you pick for depression? For anxiety? For anger? For feeling left out? For keeping secrets? For other people gossiping about you? For kids teasing you?

- Were there any listed coping skills that you had never thought of before?

- Were there any listed coping skills that you have used before? Which skills work best for you?

End That Stinkin' Thinkin' explains that shame can come from negative thinking (or "stinkin' thinkin'"). Children are introduced to the cognitive distortions of personalization, blaming, jumping to conclusions and catastrophizing. They are asked to read examples of "stinkin' thinkin'" and identify the type of cognitive distortion they represent. After completing the worksheet, the following discussion questions can be used:

- Which type of "stinkin' thinkin'" do you catch yourself using? Where do you think that came from?

- What kinds of feelings does your "stinkin' thinkin'" produce? Are those feelings comfortable?

- How could you challenge your negative thinking to produce more positive feelings (i.e. "Is this thought really true?" "What evidence is there for this thought?" etc.)? How hard will it be to break your habit of "stinkin' thinkin'?"

- How can you remind yourself to use more accurate thinking?

Self-Compassion explains that one of the cures for shame is being gentle and kind to yourself. It presents nine ways to be compassionate towards yourself and asks children to identify the ones they already practice and the ones that they would like to *start* practicing. After completing the worksheet, the following discussion questions can be used:

- Why is it important to show yourself compassion?

- What are some of the kind things that you do for yourself already?

- What are some of the kind things that you want to *start* doing for yourself? How will you remind yourself to do them?

- Can you think of other ways to be kind to yourself besides those things listed on this worksheet?

Recognizing Shame

Children of substance-abusing parents know the feeling of shame all too well. It's a feeling of embarrassment and disgrace. In order to get rid of the feeling, it's important to recognize it. Complete the following sentences in order to better understand how you experience shame.

When I feel shame, I feel it in/on the following place(s) on my body (mark it in on the body here):

Some of the things that trigger my feelings of shame are _____

_____

_____

Other feelings that I have when I feel shame are _____

_____

If I could taste shame, it would taste like _____

If I could smell shame, it would smell like _____

If I could touch shame, it would feel like _____

If I could see shame, it would look like _____

How Shame Affects Me

Shame is a feeling of extreme embarrassment or humiliation. It creates fear that keeps people from being their best. In fact, it tricks people into thinking that they are bad. Look at some of the features of shame below and check the ones that you experience. For each one that you have checked, go back and rate how strong this feels to you (1 = a little, 2 = somewhat, 3 = quite a bit, 4 = a lot).

	Put an X if yes	If yes, rate it by circling a number
I have a hard time trusting people.		1 2 3 4
I get really angry when someone corrects me or criticizes me.		1 2 3 4
I am always apologizing for something.		1 2 3 4
I feel like other kids are against me or don't like me.		1 2 3 4
I don't like to invite other kids over to my house.		1 2 3 4
I don't like myself; I don't feel like I am as good as other people.		1 2 3 4
I feel lonely.		1 2 3 4
I have secrets about myself or my family.		1 2 3 4
I feel like I have to be perfect.		1 2 3 4

Finding Coping Skills

Listed below on the left are some of the things that can happen with shame—things that create shame and things that are a consequence of shame. Scattered around on the page are positive coping skills you can use when these things happen. Draw lines from each shame event/behavior to the coping skill you think would work best for that type of shame event/behavior.

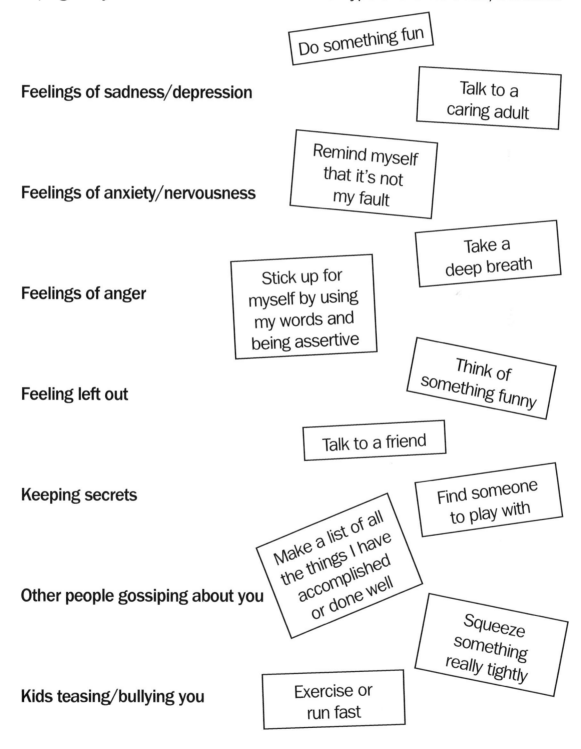

Do something fun

Feelings of sadness/depression

Talk to a caring adult

Remind myself that it's not my fault

Feelings of anxiety/nervousness

Take a deep breath

Stick up for myself by using my words and being assertive

Feelings of anger

Think of something funny

Feeling left out

Talk to a friend

Keeping secrets

Find someone to play with

Make a list of all the things I have accomplished or done well

Other people gossiping about you

Squeeze something really tightly

Kids teasing/bullying you

Exercise or run fast

End That Stinkin' Thinkin'

Feelings of shame can come from thinking mistakes or "stinkin' thinkin.'" Four kinds of "stinkin' thinkin'" include personalization, blaming, jumping to conclusions and catastrophizing.

- **Personalization**—thinking that everything other people think or do or say is because of you in some way.
- **Blaming**—believing that other people are to blame when you feel bad.
- **Jumping to conclusions**—believing something without proof.
- **Catastrophizing**—exaggerating a simple event.

Look at each statement below and circle the kind of stinkin' thinkin' it represents.

1. "It's my fault that my parent drinks and/or uses drugs."

Personalization   Blaming   Jumping to conclusions   Catastrophizing

2. "It's time for recess. No one's going to want to play with me after they saw my dad last night."

Personalization   Blaming   Jumping to conclusions   Catastrophizing

3. "I failed my spelling test. Now I'm going to fail third grade."

Personalization   Blaming   Jumping to conclusions   Catastrophizing

4. "I wouldn't have yelled at you if you hadn't made me."

Personalization   Blaming   Jumping to conclusions   Catastrophizing

Which type of stinkin' thinkin' do you find yourself using?

_____

How do you use it? Give an example.

_____

What do you need to tell yourself that is a better way of thinking?

_____

Self-Compassion

One of the cures for shame is self-compassion—or gentle care and kindness towards yourself. Listed below are some ways to have self-compassion. Circle the ones that you already do and color in the ones that you would like to *start* doing in your favorite color.

When I'm feeling down I do something nice for myself.

I forgive myself when I make mistakes.

I'm patient with myself when I'm learning new things.

If I fail at something, I remind myself that lots of other people have experienced failure as well.

If someone says mean things to me I try not to take it personally.

If I'm feeling tense, I take time to relax.

I make sure that I eat healthy foods and get plenty of rest.

If I'm bored, I find something to do.

If I want attention from someone and can't get it, I go to others to get what I need.

CHAPTER 3
Letting Go of Control

Introduction

Many children of substance-abusing parents blame themselves for their parent's substance abuse. They try to control the drinking/drug use by making good grades, keeping the house immaculate, or withdrawing, hoping not to create a disturbance. Very few children realize that they neither caused nor can they change a parent's substance problem (American Academy of Experts in Traumatic Stress 2012).

Control can become a major issue for many children of substance-abusing parents. This begins as a coping mechanism in a chaotic and unpredictable environment but, because of its rigidity, it can have maladaptive consequences (Markowitz 2013). In fact, one of the Adult Children of Alcoholics' published 14 traits of an adult child of an alcoholic (called "The Laundry List") states, "We have an overdeveloped sense of responsibility, and it is easier for us to be concerned with others rather than ourselves" (Adult Children of Alcoholics World Service Organization 1978). Children in substance-abusing families have a great deal of anxiety and sometimes spend a great deal of energy trying to control or eliminate their parents' use of drugs or alcohol.

Frequently, substance-abusing parents are unable to care for their children's needs and many of their own needs and, consequently, create a role reversal where children take responsibility for parents and themselves. This is called parentification—a phenomenon that has been found among children of addicted parents (Backett-Milburn *et al.* 2008; Grella and Greenwell 2006; Tracy and Martin 2007). These children come to feel responsible for running the family. When a child takes on parental responsibilities, it brings order back into the family but at the cost of a child's increased rigidity and overdeveloped sense of control (Pasternak and Schier 2012). Research shows that girls are at higher risk for parentification than boys and have a stronger "depressive affect" from that parentification (Grella and Greenwell 2006; Stein, Rotheram-Borus and Lester 2007).

Best Practices and Treatment Recommendations

Although children in substance-abusing homes cannot control their parents' drinking and drug use, they can learn to cope with it. One method of coping is called *adaptive distancing*—healthy emotional detachment from parents' problems. Detaching while remaining concerned (embracing ambivalence) has been shown to be an important part of children's adjustment in the face of dysfunction (Mylant *et al.* 2002). Rubin (1996) described it as:

> the ability to hold onto a self, even in the face of the assaults they suffered—make it possible to stand back and observe the fray without getting bogged down in it. They may have been pained, angered and frightened by the events of their lives, but they retained enough distance not to get caught in endlessly blaming themselves. (p.225)

In related research, *psychological distance* appears to play an important role in facilitating adaptive self-reflection (vs. maladaptive self-reflection/rumination) (Ayduk and Kross 2010; Kross 2009). *Psychological distance* is the ability to minimize people's egocentric experience of a situation which may be helpful for children of substance-abusing parents.

There is a scarcity of research addressing treatment approaches for hypervigilance, control and parentification in children of substance-abusing parents. However, in related research, adolescents who successfully coped with emotionally disturbed parents were able to distinguish between themselves and their parents' illnesses and, consequently, realized that they did not cause the illnesses (Beardslee and Podorefsky 1988). In the same way, it is important for children from chemically dependent homes also to know that they did not cause their parents' drug and alcohol problems and certainly cannot change them.

Acceptance is a significant predictor of psychological functioning in various populations (Hayes *et al.* 2006). For many years 12-step recovery programs have used the Serenity Prayer as a reminder of the importance of acceptance. Trying to fight against the way of things only leads to suffering.

Finally, beliefs about control and self-blame certainly qualify as thinking errors. Cognitive therapy has been shown to be an effective treatment approach for a plethora of emotional and behavioral problems. Identifying cognitive distortions or irrational beliefs (such as being able to control a parent's drinking) and changing those unhelpful thoughts to realistic ones is important.

General Suggestions

- Continuously remind children that they didn't cause their parents' problems; they can't cure them; and they can't control them.

- Encourage children to be open-minded about thoughts and opinions expressed in the group—teach them how to "agree to disagree."

- Model curiosity and open-mindedness as children present ideas and share feelings.

- Model non-defensiveness if children become angry with you or if you make a mistake.

- Be willing to change plans during the group if needed. Draw attention to this and verbalize how you are coping with the change (letting go of control).

- Challenge any thinking errors or irrational thinking that you hear children verbalize. Ask if the thought is really true; if there is evidence of it.

Script

"Many children who have a parent who drinks too much alcohol or uses mind-altering drugs think that they are to blame or that they should try to help their parent stop. Neither of those things are true. You are *not* to blame for your parent's drinking or using drugs, and you *cannot* make her/him stop. You cannot control what your parent does. You can only control yourself.

Don't try to be perfect and don't try to hide your parent's alcohol or drugs. You did not cause her/his disease and you are not the reason that she/he continues to drink or get high.

You may worry about your parent, of course, but try to take a step back and let her/him go through what she/he needs to go through so that she/he may want to get help some day. But remember that her/his problem is their problem—not yours."

Activities

(1) CREATING WITHOUT CONTROL

OBJECTIVE
To increase flexibility and reduce the need for control.

MATERIALS
Shaving cream, food coloring, paint tray liners, popsicle sticks and paper.

DIRECTIONS
Explain to the group that many beautiful and interesting things can happen when we let go of control and that this activity will demonstrate that fact. Give each child a paint tray, a popsicle stick and a piece of paper. Spray shaving cream into each child's plastic container and direct them to drip food coloring (not too much!) onto the shaving cream. Next, direct them to gently run a popsicle stick through the shaving cream a few times in order to mix some of the colors together. Then have them gently place their piece

of paper into the foam and pull the paper out. Scrape off any excess shaving cream to reveal a marbleized brightly colored picture.

FOLLOW-UP DISCUSSION QUESTIONS

- How did it feel to have no control over how the painting turned out?

- While you were making it, were you *curious* about how it would turn out?

- How is curiosity better than control?

- What other things in your life have you been able to be curious about rather than try to control them?

(2) LETTING GO

OBJECTIVE
To visualize letting go.

MATERIALS
Helium balloons and wide ended markers.

DIRECTIONS
Explain that letting go of trying to change other people is a freeing experience. Give each child a helium balloon (have a couple extra on hand in case any pop during the exercise). Direct them to write down a trait or a habit that they have been trying to change in someone else on their balloon (e.g. getting a parent to quit drinking or using; getting a sibling to quit tattling, etc.). Then go outside and ask the children to imagine letting go of trying to change their person as they let go of their balloons and watch them float upwards.

FOLLOW-UP DISCUSSION QUESTIONS

- What did you think about as you let go of your balloon? How did it feel?

- Could you really imagine letting go of trying to change your person?

- What would letting go of trying to change someone else look like in real life? What would you be doing differently?

- What might get in the way of you being able to let go? How will you handle that?

(3) DISTANCING

OBJECTIVE
To experience the advantages of distancing.

MATERIALS
A large picture or poster.

DIRECTIONS
Explain that sometimes we have to back up (get some distance) from a situation in order to get a better understanding of it. Hold up a large picture or poster and have each child stand right up against it (with noses almost touching it) and look at it. Then have them take one step backwards and look at it. Then have them stand on the other side of the room and look at it.

FOLLOW-UP DISCUSSION QUESTIONS

- What did you see when you stood right up against the picture? What did you see when you took a step back? What did you see when you stood across the room from it?

- Which position gave you a better understanding of what the picture really looked like?

- Do you think that a person can be too close to a situation and not really see the whole picture?

- What are some ways people need to "step back" in life?

(4) PADDLING UPSTREAM

OBJECTIVE
To physically experience efforts that are futile.

MATERIALS
Enough folding chairs for everyone in the group.

DIRECTIONS
Prior to the activity, place pairs of chairs in a line. Direct children to sit in the chairs and explain that they are going to pretend to be in a row boat (or a large boat with paddles). After everyone is seated, hand each one an invisible paddle. When everyone has received their "paddle," direct them to start paddling *upstream*. As they are role playing this, describe how strong the "current" is and how much strain it takes to paddle against the stream. Make sure that everyone is straining as they pretend to paddle upstream. Do this for several minutes and then tell them that, despite their good efforts, their boat did not really move anywhere. Then direct everyone to turn their

chairs around in the opposite direction. Explain that they are now floating *down*stream. As they don't need to paddle, have them put their "paddles" in their laps. Describe how they are moving down the river and enjoying the ride; how they can look at the trees and wild flowers on either side of the river. Continue to describe their floating experience for several minutes.

FOLLOW-UP DISCUSSION QUESTIONS

- Was it easier to go upstream or downstream?

- Which was more relaxing? Which one wore you out more?

- What could you do while you were "floating" instead of "paddling?"

- How is trying to change someone like paddling upstream? How is accepting that person like floating downstream?

(5) CRYSTAL BALL

OBJECTIVE
To recognize that change is inevitable and that it can be coped with.

MATERIALS
Paper, pencils and markers.

DIRECTIONS
Explain that changes can be difficult and create feelings of being out of control. But it can be helpful to predict some of the challenges and identify coping skills. Direct children to draw a large circle on their papers. Then ask them to draw anywhere from one to three changes that may occur in their lives over the next three months (e.g. summer vacation, a move, grade level change, etc.). After the drawings are completed, ask children to predict the feelings that these changes might produce and how they might manage those feelings. Then direct them to write their coping skills inside the circle.

FOLLOW-UP DISCUSSION QUESTIONS

- What are some of the changes that you predicted? Which ones might be the most difficult? Which ones might be easy?

- What kinds of coping skills did you come up with? Can you think of any more?

- How does it feel to know that you have a plan for your feelings? How will this help in making your changes?

- If a change happens in your life suddenly (and you don't have time to plan for it) can you use any of your coping skills?

Worksheet Discussion Questions

Do I Smell Some Stinkin' Thinkin'? lists nine thinking errors (or "stinkin' thinkin'") around the need for control. Children are asked to identify the ones that they have and to write down a more reasonable or accurate way of thinking. After completing the worksheet, the following discussion questions can be used:

- How many thinking errors or stinkin' thinkin' items did you recognize as something you have thought?

- What feelings do you have when you are thinking those thoughts?

- What feelings do you think you would have if you used the more reasonable and accurate thoughts? Do your feelings change when your thoughts change?

- What are some ways that you can catch any stinkin' thinkin' and change it?

The Serenity Prayer quotes the Serenity Prayer used in many of the 12-step recovery programs and asks children to make a list of things they *can't* control and a list of things they *can* control. Although the "prayer" addresses God, many from a wide variety of religions find meaning in it, including those who do not claim any organized religion. After completing the worksheet, the following discussion questions can be used:

- Have you heard of the Serenity Prayer before? Do you understand what it means?

- What do you think *acceptance* means?

- Why do you think someone would have to pray that prayer?

- Looking over your two lists, what are some of your thoughts or observations about what you wrote?

What I Can Count On and What I Can't Count On asks children to think about their substance-abusing parent and to make two lists—one of the things they *can* count on from that parent and the other of the things they *can't* count on from that parent. After completing the worksheet, the following discussion questions can be used:

- Looking over your two lists, what are some of your thoughts or observations?

- Are there some things on the "Can't Count On" side that you wish you *could* count on? How can you let that go or accept that you can't count on them?

- What are some of the things you *can* count on and how can you make yourself think about those more?

- Do you think that other kids of substance-abusing parents have similar lists of things they can count on and things they can't count on?

An Evaluation of My Openness asks children to consider eight openness/flexibility behaviors (the opposite of control) and to rate themselves on each one. After completing the worksheet, the following discussion questions can be used:

- Which of the items were you strongest in? Which do you have the most trouble with?

- What do you think are the benefits of being open and flexible?

- Why do you think it's important to be curious?

- Can you talk about a time when you were able to agree to disagree with someone? What was that like?

Things I've Let Go Of invites children to consider things that they have already let go of in their lives (e.g. pacifiers as babies, training wheels on two-wheeled bikes, etc.) and to draw pictures of these. After completing the worksheet, the following discussion questions can be used:

- What are some of the things you've let go of in your life?

- How were you able to do that? Was it difficult?

- Why did you let go of them?

- What are some things you need to let go of now in your life? (Things to consider: letting go of needing to be right, letting go of blaming others, letting go of self-defeating self-talk, letting go of fears, etc.)

Do I Smell Some Stinkin' Thinkin'?

When people's thoughts cause them to feel stressed it's usually because they have "stinkin' thinkin'" or thinking errors. Listed below is some "stinkin' thinkin'." Pick the thinking errors that you have frequently, draw arrows from them to the lines below and write a more reasonable and accurate way of thinking. (Example: You could change "I never do anything right" to "I may not always do things right but I do several things pretty well.")

- There must be a way I can turn my parent around.

- If I quit trying, I might lose my parent.

- My parent is so irresponsible she/he could never do it on her/his own.

- My family would be so much better if they only listened to me.

- I must solve every family problem.

- Only I can solve these family problems.

- If I don't solve these problems, I'm a failure.

- If I don't make things better around here, I'll go crazy.

- My parent will blame me if I don't take care of her/him.

_____

_____

_____

_____

_____

_____

_____

The Serenity Prayer

"God, grant me the serenity to accept the things I cannot change,

The courage to change the things I can,

And the wisdom to know the difference."

Alcoholics Anonymous and many 12-step programs use the Serenity Prayer because it is so helpful. It reminds people that they can't control everything. In the columns below, list things that you can control (mostly things about yourself!) and things that you cannot control (mostly things about others!).

WHAT I CAN CONTROL   WHAT I CANNOT CONTROL

What I Can Count On and What I Can't Count On

In every relationship there are things you can count on and things you can't count on. For example, you may be able to count on a friend to think of fun activities to do, but not count on her/him to be on time. Or you may be able to count on your teacher to grade your homework accurately, but not count on her/him always to remain patient when the class is noisy. Now think about your parent who is addicted to drugs or alcohol. What are some things you can count on her/him for and what are some things you cannot count on her/him for? List them below.

WHAT I CAN COUNT ON   WHAT I CANNOT COUNT ON

An Evaluation of My Openness

Being open and flexible is important for both happiness and being able to let go of control. Measure your overall openness below by shading in the rulers to the right of each statement. Higher numbers and more shading means more agreement with the statement. Lower numbers and less shading means less agreement.

1. I am open to new ideas.

1 2 3 4 5 6 7 8 9 10 11 12

2. I am curious about people and the world around me.

1 2 3 4 5 6 7 8 9 10 11 12

3. I am OK when things are vague or uncertain.

1 2 3 4 5 6 7 8 9 10 11 12

4. I go after new knowledge and experiences.

1 2 3 4 5 6 7 8 9 10 11 12

5. I am accepting of other people's ideas even when they differ from my own.

1 2 3 4 5 6 7 8 9 10 11 12

6. I can see both sides of a story.

1 2 3 4 5 6 7 8 9 10 11 12

7. I like a variety of activities.

1 2 3 4 5 6 7 8 9 10 11 12

8. I like going to new places.

1 2 3 4 5 6 7 8 9 10 11 12

Which of the things listed above would you like to work on? _____

_____

How will you work on it? What is your plan? _____

_____

Things I've Let Go Of

Everyone has let go of things in their lives—even kids. For example, if you loved a pacifier as a baby, you probably don't still use one. You let go of it! Draw pictures of four things that you have let go of in your life.

CHAPTER 4

Understanding and Managing Feelings

Introduction

Children of substance-abusing parents are subjected to a greater number of expressions of anger and, consequently, exhibit more intense emotional reactions themselves (Ballard and Cummings 1990). Children can simultaneously feel unjustly treated and enraged at their addicted parent while also feeling worried about and fearful of losing her/him. Children often have mixed and unidentified feelings of shame, guilt, embarrassment, confusion, anger, depression, anxiety, isolation and helplessness.

Black (2010) states that children of substance-abusing parents must numb their feelings in order to survive the constant pain of living with substance abuse. She contends that children must shut down their feelings in order to avoid being overwhelmed by them. In addition to numbing negative feelings, Markowitz (2013) suggests that children learn to shut down positive feelings as well, as these often lead to disappointment. She further describes how children must become overly attuned to their parents' emotional states resulting in a poor recognition of their own emotions.

While not specifically targeted to children of addicted parents, Smith and Walden (1999) found that children who were exposed to more negative attitudes show more negative emotions and have poorer emotional understanding and weaker coping skills. Research with adult children of alcoholics has found that they have fewer and less effective coping strategies than adults who were not raised with alcoholic parents (Hall 2007; Hansson *et al.* 2006). In dealing with stressful emotions, they use more avoidance coping strategies (e.g. smoking and drinking) and fewer self-sufficient or socially supported coping (Klostermann *et al.* 2011).

Research has shown that children with lower emotional intelligence are more likely to have emotional and behavioral problems (Poulou 2014). The abilities to recognize, understand, express and manage emotions help control impulsive reactions, develop healthy relationships and become successful in school and work

(Elias and Weissberg 2000; Payton *et al.* 2000). Indeed, "emotional intelligence" is an important predictor of personal adjustment and social behavior, as emotions are an integral part of decisional processes and cognitive problem solving (Mayer, Roberts and Barsade 2008).

Best Practices and Treatment Recommendations

There is clear evidence that emotional intelligence training programs and social-emotional skills training programs improve psychological and social functioning for children of all ages, including many at-risk groups. Research has shown that participation in emotional intelligence programs reduces aggression, anxiety, stress, depression and somatization, while improving problem solving, empathy and self-esteem (Brackett *et al.* 2012; Conner and Fraser 2011; Ruiz-Aranda *et al.* 2012; Ulutas and Omeroglu 2007).

There are many evidence-based curricula that enhance children's emotional and social competence both at the universal (prevention) level and at the selective (at-risk) level. Core to all of the social/emotional learning programs is identifying and naming feelings, or "emotional literacy." Not only does naming feelings create a better understanding of emotions and improve self-awareness, it also reduces emotional reactivity in the amygdala, the part of the brain responsible for fight–flight–freeze reactions (Lieberman *et al.* 2007). Naming feelings therefore may be the first step in self-regulation and emotion management.

Many emotional literacy programs also focus on understanding and regulating emotions. Understanding emotions involves recognizing nonverbal cues that are produced in one's body, understanding the information that emotions convey, and the impact that feelings expression has on others. Regulating emotions includes utilization of cognitive techniques (changing self-talk) and behavioral techniques (distraction or calming activities).

Another promising intervention for emotion regulation is Dialectical Behavioral Therapy (DBT). While no studies to date have examined the results of DBT with children of substance-abusing parents, it has been used with emotionally dysregulated adolescents with positive outcomes (Fleischhaker *et al.* 2011; McDonell *et al.* 2010). DBT utilizes the techniques of mindfulness, acting opposite, distraction and self-talk.

General Suggestions

- Keep feelings words posters hung in the room for reference.

- Model naming feelings. As appropriate, amplify the use of feelings words to describe your own emotional state.

- Reflect children's nonverbal feelings cues by using feelings words ("You're sad about that," "You look really happy today," "You seemed angry when she said that to you," etc.).

- Remind children that no feeling is a bad feeling.
- If a child's emotions start to escalate at any time during the sessions, have her/him focus and meditate on a small object in the room for at least one minute or distract her/him with a special job to do for you.

Script

"When you live with a parent who is stuck on drugs or alcohol, you can have lots of strong feelings. Sometimes it's confusing because you can feel two or more feelings at the same time. You can feel love and hate at the same time; you can feel worried and angry at the same time; you can feel scared and ashamed at the same time. Sometimes you may feel your feelings so strongly that you think you're going to pop and other times you may not feel anything at all.

Some of the feelings that kids with addicted parents have talked about are mistrust, shame, confusion, guilt, fear, self-doubt, disappointment and anger but there are lots more. It's helpful to be able to figure out what you are feeling and to talk about it. During our time together we're going to talk about all of our many, many feelings. While no feeling is bad, it's good to be the boss of your feelings rather than having your feelings be the boss of you. What other feelings can you name?"

Activities

(1) NAME THAT FEELING

OBJECTIVE
To increase the association of nonverbal body cues and feelings words.

MATERIALS
None.

DIRECTIONS
Explain that our bodies give us clues about what we are feeling. If we listen to our bodies we can identify our feelings. Then tell the children that you will be reading out a list of three body sensations for one feeling. They will act out the three body sensations and then try to guess the feeling.

Frown with your eyebrows.

Bite down hard with your teeth.

Clench your fists.

ANSWER: Angry.

Hang your head.

Slump your shoulders.

Stick out your bottom lip.

ANSWER: Sad.

Frown with your eyebrows.

Look up with just your eyes.

Scratch your head.

ANSWER: Confused.

Put your arms up in the air.

Make a big smile.

Jump up and down.

ANSWER: Excited.

Rest your head on your hand.

Look up with just your eyes.

Make a big sigh.

ANSWER: Bored.

FOLLOW-UP DISCUSSION QUESTIONS

- How easy or hard was it to figure out the feelings with the body and face gestures?
- Which one was the easiest? Which one was the hardest?
- Can you describe any other feelings and their body senses?
- What did you learn about feelings from this exercise?

(2) FEELINGS LINE

OBJECTIVE

To increase emotional literacy and to understand the varying degrees of a feeling.

MATERIALS

Masking tape.

DIRECTIONS

Explain that feelings can be mild, medium or strong; that different feeling levels often have different words that describe them. Then tape a five-foot piece of masking tape across the floor. Identify one end of the tape as very mild and the other end as very strong and the center as medium with all the other degrees in between. Read each of the following feelings and have the children place themselves along the line as to how strong they believe the word is. (There are four feelings families represented.)

Angry	Happy	Sad	Scared
Aggravated	Content	Miserable	Terrified
Annoyed	Ecstatic	Gloomy	Nervous
Furious	Excited	Discouraged	Worried
Enraged	Pleased	Depressed	Anxious

FOLLOW-UP DISCUSSION QUESTIONS

- Did you learn any new feelings words from this activity? What were they?

- How does it help you to know different feelings words for the different degrees of a feeling?

- Did everyone agree on how mild or strong a particular feeling word was? Why do you think that was?

- Do you usually experience your feelings at a mild, medium or strong level?

(3) DIFFICULT FEELINGS

OBJECTIVE

To identify difficult feelings and practice talking about them.

MATERIALS

Paper, pencils, crayons or markers and copies of a feelings words list.

DIRECTIONS

Explain to the group that having a parent with drug or alcohol problems often means that they have feelings that are hard to talk about—feelings that may be painful, frightening or overwhelming. Then provide each child with a feelings words list, a piece of paper and a pen or pencil; instruct them to write down five of *their* difficult feelings on one side of the paper. Then ask them to select one of those feelings and, on the other side of the paper, to draw a situation where they felt one of those feelings. Share pictures but allow children to decline if they so choose.

FOLLOW-UP DISCUSSION QUESTIONS

- How easy or hard was it for you to draw a picture of a time when you had one of those difficult feelings?

- What makes some feelings harder to talk about than others?

- How does your family handle it when you try to talk about difficult feelings?

- Since we did this exercise, do you think it will be easier to talk about your difficult feelings the next time you experience them?

- Besides talking, what else can you do to make yourself feel better when you have difficult feelings?

(4) COPING SKILLS BINGO

OBJECTIVE

To increase familiarity with different kinds of coping skills.

MATERIALS

Copies of Bingo cards from Appendix B and Bingo chips.

DIRECTIONS

Prior to the group, make copies of the Bingo cards in Appendix B. There are six different cards and, while all of them have the same coping skills, they are arranged differently so that there should only be one winner. Explain that you will be calling out coping skills (see list below) and players should find them on their cards and cover them with chips. As soon as someone has five chips in a line, she/he should shout out, "Bingo!"

Exercise	Relax	List things you are grateful for	Listen to music
Clean something	Play a sport	Think of puffy white clouds	Talk to an adult
Dance	Take a bath	Think of a peaceful place	Blow bubbles
Count to 100	Play with clay	Say a tongue-twister five times	Talk to a friend
Make up a game	Play with water	Play a musical instrument	Sing
Work in a garden	Write a letter	Spend time with a pet	Draw a picture

FOLLOW-UP DISCUSSION QUESTIONS

- Which Bingo coping skills have you used? When have you used them?

- Which Bingo coping skills have you seen others use? How did it work for them?

- Of the Bingo coping skills that you *haven't* tried before, which one would you *like* to try? When could you use it?

- When do you need coping skills the most?

- Which of the Bingo coping skills do you think will work best for you?

(5) CALMING COLLAGE

OBJECTIVE

To provide a calming coping strategy for future use.

MATERIALS

Construction paper, scissors, glue, cut-out pictures and words from magazines and newspapers that depict calm/relaxation/safety (try to find things that use all five senses—pictures of things that look, taste, smell, feel and sound calming), and old scraps of wallpaper, foils or other decorative papers.

DIRECTIONS

Explain that when distressing feelings get very intense it can be helpful to have something calming to focus or meditate on. Instruct the children to select a piece of construction paper to use as a background for their collage. Then direct them to select pictures and words that represent calm/relaxation/safety for them. Have them glue these to their piece of construction paper and decorate with old scraps of wallpaper, foils or other decorative papers. Invite children to take these home and post them in a place where they can access them as needed. (If a child declines to take her/his collage home, respect her/his wishes and ask where she/he might want to keep it.)

OPTIONAL: Play calming music while children are assembling their collages.

FOLLOW-UP DISCUSSION QUESTIONS

- What were your feelings as you glued pictures to your Calming Collage?

- Which senses do you have in your pictures (look, taste, smell, feel and sound)?

- If you focus on your collage for a few seconds, what kinds of thoughts and feelings do you have?

- Under what circumstances do you think that you will be able to use your Calming Collage at home?

Worksheet Discussion Questions

Emotion Houses has six different feeling category descriptions put in "houses." It asks children to identify which feelings words belong in which house. After completing the worksheet, the following discussion questions can be used:

- Were there any feelings words that went into the same house you were surprised about?

- Can you think of any other feelings that might go in one of the houses?

- Which house's feelings are you most comfortable with?

- Which house's feelings are you most *un*comfortable with?

Feel-ometer asks children to identify three feelings that they have a difficult time talking about and a situation where they felt those feelings. Then they are asked to measure the strength of that feeling by coloring in its "temperature" on a thermometer. After completing the worksheet, the following discussion questions can be used:

- How difficult was it to admit difficult feelings?

- How difficult was it to remember the situation that triggered those feelings?

- Has anyone ever told you not to feel a certain way? What did you think of that?

- Who is someone in your family who you can talk to about your difficult feelings? Who is someone *outside* your family who you can talk to about your difficult feelings?

Walking Through the Valley shows two mountains and one valley. Children are directed to write down two mountain top (happy) experiences and one valley (sad) experience. They are then asked to identify ways that they have grown from their valley experience. After completing the worksheet, the following discussion questions can be used:

- What were your mountain top experiences? What other feelings besides happy did you feel during those experiences?

- What was your valley experience? What other feelings besides sad did you feel during that experience?

- Do you think that everyone has both mountain top and valley experiences?

- More things grow in the valleys than on the mountains. How have you grown from your valley experience?

Underneath the Angry Feelings asks children to list five situations when they felt angry. They are then asked to look more deeply into those events and identify other underlying feelings by checking off the appropriate triggering feelings. After completing the worksheet, the following discussion questions can be used:

- Were you surprised that other feelings can trigger anger?

- Which feeling(s) did you mark the most? Talk about that feeling and how it triggers your anger.

- What are other situations that tempt you to feel that anger-triggering feeling?

- How can you calm yourself when you feel anger and the other anger-triggering emotions?

Changing My Stinkin' Thinkin' presents children with the kinds of positive and negative thoughts they can choose to think when they are feeling an intense emotion. They are asked to color the negative ones red and the positive ones blue. After completing the worksheet, the following discussion questions can be used:

- What happens to feelings when you think negative thoughts?

- What happens to feelings when you think positive thoughts?

- How can you get yourself to switch to positive thoughts if you catch yourself thinking negatively?

- Who do you know who manages her/his feelings well? What kind of things do you think she/he thinks?

Emotion Houses

Look at the descriptions of the different Emotion Houses. Using the feelings words below, write each one in one of the six "houses" where it belongs. More than one feeling can go in the same house.

angry	anxious	amused	affection	calm
annoyed	helpless	joyful	powerless	embarrassed
sad	excited	friendly	content	mad
worried	hurt	happy	loved	relaxed

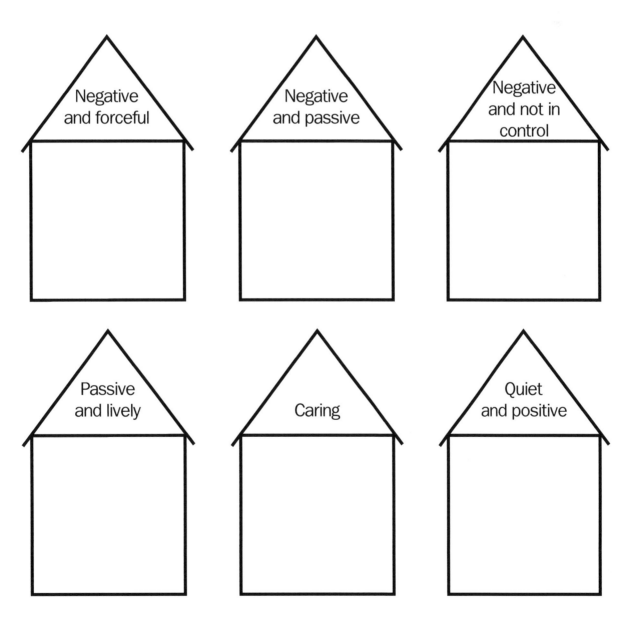

Feel-ometer

Some feelings are harder to talk about than others. These include feeling sad, stupid, worried, helpless, put down, left out, embarrassed, nervous and many others. In the FEELING spaces below, write down three feelings that you have a hard time talking about. Then, in the SITUATION space, write down a time when you felt that feeling. After that, color in the thermometer to show how "hot" (or strong) that feeling was during the situation that you identified.

FEELING: _____

SITUATION: _____

_____

FEELING: _____

SITUATION: _____

_____

FEELING: _____

SITUATION: _____

_____

Walking Through the Valley

People talk about "mountain top" experiences as being high (happy) points in their lives and "valleys" as being low (sad) points in their lives. Write or draw two high points in your life on the mountains and then write or draw one low point in your life on the valley below. Then answer the questions.

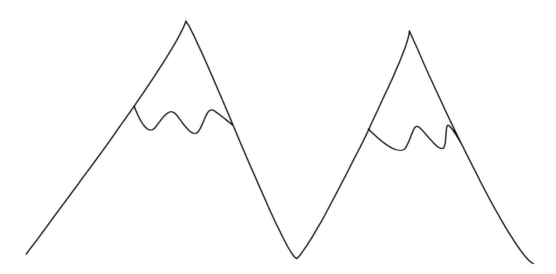

Mountain top experiences are more fun than valley experiences but in the valley is where things grow. List the ways you have grown from your valley experience:

1.

2.

3.

Underneath the Angry Feelings

While anger is just a feeling, it can create problems if kids act out on it. Understanding anger can be helpful in managing it. Because anger is often triggered by other feelings it is considered a *secondary* emotion. Write down five situations when you felt angry. Then, next to each situation, put an X in the boxes under the other feelings words that might have triggered your anger in each of the situations.

	Embarrassed	Stupid	Disappointed	Cheated	Powerless	Left out	Confused
1. _____							
2. _____							
3. _____							
4. _____							
5. _____							

Which feeling did you mark the most? _____

What do you think that means? _____

_____

Changing My Stinkin' Thinkin'

When your feelings get really intense and overwhelming it is often because you are thinking negative thoughts. If you can change your "stinkin' thinkin'" it can usually calm you down. Listed below are lots of different thoughts. Color the positive thoughts light blue and the negative thoughts red.

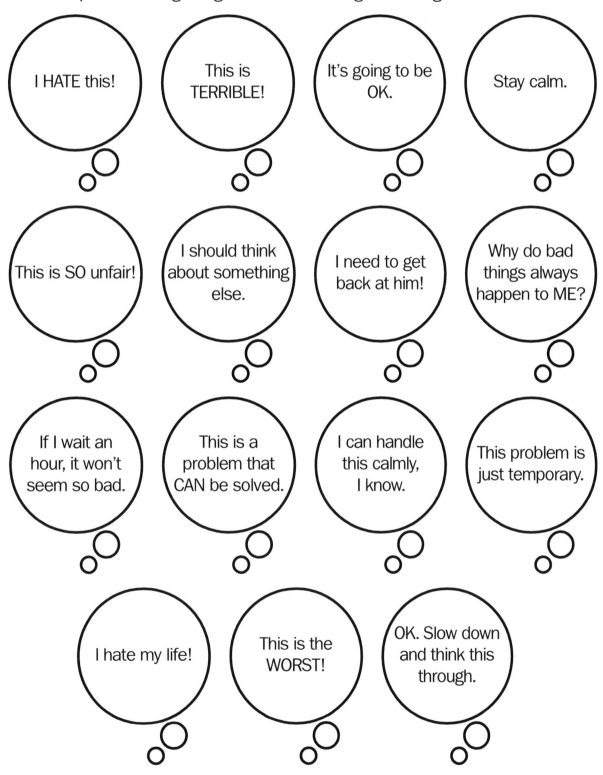

CHAPTER 5

Safety and Self-Care

Introduction

Research suggests that the first use of alcohol and other drugs is starting at younger and younger ages (Stoltenberg *et al.* 1999). This early experimentation and addiction impairs emotional development and maturation—critical prerequisites to good parenting. When parents have substance abuse problems, alcohol and drugs become a priority, causing them to be less emotionally and physically available for their children. In addition, large numbers of substance-abusing parents have neglect, physical abuse and/or sexual abuse histories. Their own traumatic childhoods and early substance abuse make them poorly equipped for effective parenting, thereby putting their own children at risk for inadequate care (Bays 1992).

Indeed, children of substance-abusing parents are more likely to be the recipients of physical, sexual or emotional abuse and to witness family violence than children in non-substance-abusing homes (US Department of Health and Human Services, Administration for Children and Families 2002). They are also at risk when riding in cars with substance-abusing parents. In 2012, almost half of all traffic deaths in the US involved an alcohol or drug-impaired driver (US Department of Transportation 2012).

In addition to safety issues, children of substance-abusing parents also lose some of the joy of childhood. In a study by Laybourn, Brown and Hill (1996), young adults who had grown up in alcoholic homes remembered "having missed out on vital components of childhood" (p.97). Many felt they had lost opportunities for fun and laughter and that this loss had had a significant impact on their sense of identity (Velleman and Orford 1999).

Best Practices and Treatment Recommendations

Robinson (1989) recommends that children of substance-abusing parents be taught basic first aid and instructed on safety guidelines. He suggests that they be taught accident prevention, the difference between healthy and abusive touching, personal hygiene and nutrition. By learning to take good care of themselves, children recognize that they are deserving of care—that they can love and respect themselves.

In a review of sexual abuse education and body safety programs, research indicates that several programs have demonstrated children's gains in knowledge about personal safety and the importance of disclosure. These programs have taught children to resist inappropriate touching, an important skill for children who may be at risk for sexual abuse (Kenny *et al.* 2008).

Christensen (1997) interviewed children living in homes with alcohol abuse and found that children wanted a break or respite from their family problems. They expressed a desire for activities both with their families and without their families. Although not a remedy for the problems, taking a break provides renewed strength to face problems.

Wolin and Wolin (1993) found that humor is one of the seven resiliency factors used by children in troubled families. Humor is finding the comic in the tragic. It is creative—begins with play and grows into the ability to see the absurd and to laugh at one's own emotional pain.

While there are no studies that have examined play and humor as treatment techniques for children of substance-abusing parents, there is a plethora of research identifying the benefits of play and humor. Play and humor contribute to physical health and pain tolerance, emotional health, social connection and communication (Carrica 2009; Mahoney, Burroughs and Hieatt 2001; Marks-Tarlow 2012; Martin *et al.* 2003; Peterson, Park and Seligman 2006; Sprecher and Regan 2002; Tan *et al.* 2008). It also maximizes cognitive capacities, enhances creativity and supports the change process (Felices 2005; Humke and Schaefer 1996; Robinson 2010; Takahashi and Inoue 2009). Humor also creates an adaptive detachment from problems and is an effective way of coping—much needed for children of substance abusers.

General Suggestions

- Model safety. Make sure the environment is safe and a first aid kit is available.

- If snacks are served, make sure that they are nutritious ones (fruit, carrots, cheese and crackers, etc.). Talk about healthy choices.

- Collect jokes, cartoons, YouTube videos to share.

- Keep toys and props available for spontaneous acts of silliness.

- Create a laughter bulletin board where everyone can contribute cartoons, baby pictures, jokes, etc.

Script

"Staying safe and taking care of yourself means you'll be able to have more fun. It's no fun being hurt or scared! Sometimes, when parents drink or get high on drugs, their behavior can feel scary. But you can learn to take care of yourself by going to your bedroom, calling someone you trust, and not getting into a car with anyone who is drunk or high. (If you *have* to ride with someone who is drunk or high—but you really should try not to—try to sit in the middle of the back seat where it is safest.)

It's also important to learn other ways to stay safe—at home, at school, in the community and on the internet. It's helpful to know what to do to stay protected *wherever* you are!

Along with staying safe, it's valuable to know how to take care of yourself when you're feeling stressed or sad or overwhelmed. A good start is by eating well, getting exercise, getting plenty of rest and having fun. Yes, I said *fun*. Did you know that it is *good* for you to laugh and play? It is! What are some ways that you stay safe and have fun?"

Activities

(1) SEEKING SAFETY GAME

OBJECTIVE
To identify the many domains and the many strategies needed to stay safe.

MATERIALS
Colored index cards and pen.

DIRECTIONS
Prior to the group session, use several colored index cards to write down various times/places when behaving safely is important. Use only one situation per card. After you have as many cards as you would like to use, hide them around the room.

NOTE: The situation cards can be tailored to the specific needs of the children in the group; they can be general or specific. Here are a few suggestions but do not feel limited by these:

- in the sun
- on the bus
- on the playground
- taking a bath
- swimming
- cooking
- cleaning
- walking alone
- on the internet

- if someone is drinking alcohol near you

- if someone asks you to keep an uncomfortable secret

- if someone touches you in a private place

- if someone threatens to hurt you.

When ready to play the game, tell the children that the time to be safe is *all* the time. Explain that there are colored index cards hidden throughout the room. When you say, "Go!" they can begin searching for them. As soon as someone finds a card, she/he should call out, "Safe!" and everyone must go back to their seats while the person reads the card and describes at least one thing she/he could *do* to stay safe in the situation (e.g. for "In the sun," she/he could say, "Wear sun screen," "Stay in the shade as much as possible," etc.). After she/he has finished, the facilitator says, "Go!" again and children return to hunting. This is repeated until all of the cards are found. If one child is finding more than her/his fair share of cards, she/he can be encouraged to help someone else who is having a more difficult time. The game is over when all of the cards are found.

FOLLOW-UP DISCUSSION QUESTIONS

- What is something new that you learned from this game?

- Did you realize that there were so many ways to stay safe?

- What kinds of things have you done in the past to stay safe?

- What is something new that you will do to stay safe after today?

(2) GERMS BE GONE!

OBJECTIVE

To increase awareness of personal hygiene and health through hand washing.

MATERIALS

Glitter, antibacterial soap and water (at a sink).

DIRECTIONS

Explain to the group that germs cause illness and can be spread with unclean hands. And, while they may run their hands under water as a gesture to wash them, this does not really get them clean. The Center for Disease Control recommends that hands be scrubbed for 15–20 seconds with an antibacterial soap. Ask the children to pretend that the glitter pieces are germs. Then sprinkle glitter on their hands and instruct them to wash it off. (Because glitter is naturally sticky, it will take up to 30 seconds to scrub it away.)

FOLLOW-UP DISCUSSION QUESTIONS

- Were you surprised by how long it took to get the glitter off your hands? Did you realize that germs are like that?

- When should you wash your hands?

- What are other things that need to stay clean in order to be healthy?

- What keeps you (i.e. obstacles) from washing your hands the right way? How can you overcome these?

(3) SAFETY MEDITATION

OBJECTIVE

To visualize safety.

MATERIALS

None.

DESCRIPTION

Explain to the group that meditation reduces stress and improves health. Then ask them to find a comfortable seat, close their eyes (if they wish) and take a deep breath, making sure that they exhale completely. Then read the following meditation in a calm, soothing manner:

I'd like for you to think about a time and place when you've felt really safe. Take a few moments and let your mind float over some of the possibilities. Take your time. If you're having trouble remembering a time and place when you felt safe, you can fantasize about a perfectly safe place. You can include people who you trust in your place or not, depending on what feels right to you. Now take another deep breath and, as you are thinking about your safe place, look around. How does it look? What is in front of you? On either side of you? Behind you? Notice the colors and the shapes. (Pause for a few seconds.)

Now take another deep breath and listen carefully. What do you hear in your safe place? Is there more than one sound? Or only one? Notice where the sounds are coming from. Are they steady sounds or do they come and go randomly? Are they high pitched or low pitched? Take a moment and focus on the sounds in your safe place. (Pause for a few seconds.)

Take another deep breath and imagine the smells and tastes of your safe place. What does it smell and taste like? Are these familiar smells and tastes or new smells and tastes? And, finally, think about feeling—or touch. What does the air feel like in your safe place? What is the temperature? What do the objects around you feel like? Are they smooth or rough? Are they warm or cold? Spend a minute and think about the smell, the taste and the feel of your safe place. (Pause for a few seconds.)

Now take a final deep breath and open your eyes while you keep that safe feeling inside of you.

FOLLOW-UP DISCUSSION QUESTIONS

- What are some of your favorite memories of feeling safe?

- Why is it important to feel safe? What feelings do you have when you feel safe and what feelings do you have when you feel unsafe? Which is healthier? Which is happier?

- Is there anyone or any place in your life where you do *not* feel safe? What can you do about this?

- What can you do if you feel unsafe when your parent is drinking alcohol or using drugs? Where are some safe places you can go?

(4) SPEAK UP!

OBJECTIVE
To increase awareness of interpersonal dangers and to improve assertiveness skills.

MATERIALS
Dry erase board or flip chart and markers.

DIRECTIONS
Prior to meeting with the group, write a list of assertive refusal statements on a flip chart or dry erase board. Feel free to come up with your own but here are a few suggestions:

- Leave me alone.
- I'll tell.
- I'm not allowed to do that.
- No.
- I don't want to do that.
- Please don't do that.
- That makes me feel really uncomfortable.
- Stop it!
- That's not appropriate.

Explain to the group that, while most adults/adolescents are safe, there are a few people who are not safe. When those unsafe adults/adolescents ask children to do things that are not appropriate, it is OK for children to refuse. Have children take turns role playing potentially unsafe situations with one child playing the adult/adolescent and the other child playing her/himself. The child who is playing her/himself should use a three step refusal process:

1. Say "no" by using one of the statements listed on the flip chart/dry erase board or using her/his own refusal statements.
2. Move away from the problem/person.
3. Tell a trusted adult.

The following scenarios can be used or you can make up your own:

- Someone asks you if you are going to be home alone.
- An older teen asks you to touch him in a way that makes you feel uncomfortable.
- Your neighbor hugs you too long.
- A relative always walks in on you when you are in the bathroom.
- An adult offers you money to do something against the rules.
- One of your parent's friends wants to talk to you about sex every time she/he comes over.
- A relative tickles you too roughly.
- A babysitter asks you to play a game where you take your clothes off.
- A stranger tries to make you get into her/his car.
- A teacher touches you in a way that makes you feel uncomfortable.

FOLLOW-UP DISCUSSION QUESTIONS

- How did it feel to refuse in the role play?
- Children are taught to obey adults and most of the time this is a good thing. When is it OK *not* to obey adults?
- Has an adult ever asked you to keep a secret that was uncomfortable to you? What did you do?
- Have you ever refused someone in real life when you didn't feel safe? How did it work?

(5) BRING BACK SILLY

OBJECTIVE
To increase laughter and fun (to be a kid).

MATERIALS
Napkins and silly glasses.

DIRECTIONS

Explain that it is healthy and good to be silly once in a while. Research actually shows that laughter is good for you! Then tell everyone that together they are going to be the NapkinHead family. Everyone should take a napkin and poke two small holes in it to see out of. Then they should place the napkin over their face (with holes in front of their eyes) and secure it to their heads with a pair of glasses over the napkin. Then they should push part of the napkin inside their lips so that they can talk. Encourage children to interact as the NapkinHead family.

NOTE: If you need more fun for your group, other silly activities can include tongue-twisters, hula hoops, corny jokes, wearing silly hats, silly face painting, silly walks and dances, and stick-on mustaches.

FOLLOW-UP DISCUSSION QUESTIONS

- On a scale of 1–10, how much fun did you have with this activity? What other activities are this much fun or *more* fun?

- What are the names of some funny movies that you have seen?

- What feelings do you have when you are laughing and having fun?

- How can you put more fun into your life?

Worksheet Discussion Questions

Safe/Unsafe Tic-Tac-Toe asks children to look over the behaviors listed on a tic-tac-toe grid and to circle the safe ones and put an X over the unsafe ones. After completing the worksheet, the following discussion questions can be used:

- Looking at the unsafe behaviors, which ones have you done? How can you correct this?

- Looking at the safe behaviors, which ones have you done? How will you continue?

- What other safe and unsafe behaviors can you think of?

- Why is it important for you to stay safe?

LOTS of Ways to Take Care of Yourself invites children to list two ways they can take care of themselves in the areas of nutrition, sleep, physical health and emotional health. After completing the worksheet, the following discussion questions can be used:

- Of the eight behaviors that you listed (two for each of the four areas), which ones do you already do?

- Which of the eight behaviors that you listed is important for you to *start* doing? How would you do it?

- Are there other things you could be doing for yourself that you didn't list?

- What are some of the benefits of taking care of yourself?

Investigating Self-Care directs children to pretend to be investigators and to interview two well-adjusted people (perhaps one of your teachers or counselors) about the ways they take care of themselves, when they do so and how effective their self-care methods are. (If possible, it is preferable that children interview adults. However, this may not always be possible.) After completing the worksheet, the following discussion questions can be used:

- How did you decide who to interview?

- In what kinds of ways do well-adjusted people take care of themselves?

- Did you discover any new self-care plans for yourself through your investigations?

- Self-care is always important but when is it most important for you?

Self-Care Toolbox encourages children to stop and take care of themselves when stressful things happen. It directs them to write down five self-care behaviors that they can put in their Self-Care Toolbox for when they need them. After completing the worksheet, the following discussion questions can be used:

- What are the five self-care items that you put in your "Toolbox?"

- Which ones have you used in the past? How did they work?

- Which ones are things you've not tried yet but think are a good idea?

- Why is it important to take care of yourself during stressful times?

Remembering "Ha-Ha"s invites children to remember various funny things in their lives—funny people, funny movies/TV shows, funny times and funny jokes. After completing the worksheet, the following discussion questions can be used:

- How many times a day do you laugh?

- Are there any times when your family laughs together?

- Do animals ever make you laugh?

- What do you like about laughing?

Safe/Unsafe Tic-Tac-Toe

Read the safe and unsafe behaviors below. Circle the safe ones and put an X over the unsafe ones. See if you can find a tic-tac-toe!

Wearing a life jacket when swimming in the lake	Riding in a car with a driver who has been drinking alcohol or using drugs	Emailing personal information to an unknown person
Letting an adult know where you are going	Going down the slide feet first	Getting in the middle of two people in a physical fight to break it up
Helping a stranger find the owner of a lost puppy	Taking someone else's medicine	Wearing a helmet when riding a bicycle

What is another unsafe behavior? _____

_____

What is another safe behavior? _____

_____

LOTS of Ways to Take Care of Yourself

There are lots of ways to nurture or take care of yourself. Listed below are several areas of a person's life where it can be done. Under each area, list two ways you can take good care of yourself. An example is provided for you.

NUTRITION

Example: "I can avoid skipping meals."

1. _____

_____

2. _____

_____

SLEEP

1. _____

_____

2. _____

_____

PHYSICAL HEALTH

1. _____

_____

2. _____

_____

EMOTIONAL HEALTH

1. _____

   _____

2. _____

   _____

Investigating Self-Care

Pretend that you are an investigator looking for clues about self-care. Find three people who seem well adjusted and interview them about how they take care of themselves. Write down their answers.

PERSON 1

What is one way you take care of yourself? _____

_____

When do you use it? _____

_____

On a scale of 1–10 (1 = works a tiny bit; 10 = works fabulously) how well does this technique work for you? _____

PERSON 2

What is one way you take care of yourself? _____

_____

When do you use it? _____

_____

On a scale of 1–10 (1 = works a tiny bit; 10 = works fabulously) how well does this technique work for you? _____

PERSON 3

What is one way you take care of yourself? _____

_____

When do you use it? _____

_____

On a scale of 1–10 (1 = works a tiny bit; 10 = works fabulously) how well does this technique work for you? _____

Self-Care Toolbox

When stressful situations happen it's always good to stop and take care of yourself. Write down some things in the boxes below that you could do (or put in your Self-Care Toolbox) when feeling stressed (examples: sit in nature, listen to music, etc.).

Remembering "Ha-Ha"s

Humor helps you find something funny in a situation or in yourself. Even when things seem really bad, if you can find something amusing in it, it will relieve tension and make the situation seem better. Listed below are some questions about things that have made you laugh. Answer each one.

Who is the funniest person you know? _____

What makes her/him funny? _____

_____

When did you laugh until you almost cried or peed your pants? _____

_____

What is the funniest movie or TV show you've ever seen? _____

_____

What was one of the funniest parts? _____

_____

What is a favorite joke?_____

_____

CHAPTER 6
Building Relationships

Introduction

Parental substance abuse can sometimes result in the temporary physical loss of parents due to divorce, imprisonment, time away for rehabilitation or removal due to child welfare proceedings. Kroll (2004) identified children's fears about their parents "disappearing" unexpectedly. Both the *reality* of being abandoned and the *fear* of being abandoned were poignant issues for children of substance-abusing parents. Children reported feelings of isolation, loneliness and a sense that there was no one to turn to and no one to trust.

Parents' problems with substance abuse can also result in an emotional absence which, during children's early development, can contribute to children's insecure attachments (Flores 2001; Howe *et al.* 1999). Substance abuse makes it difficult for parents to read an infant's cues because of delayed response times and altered perceptions from substances, producing these insecure attachments. Research suggests that unavailable or inconsistent caregivers may lead children to repeat patterns of poor relationships (Kelley *et al.* 2004) in addition to problems with externalizing behaviors, anxiety and social cognition problems (Colonnesi *et al.* 2011; Fearon *et al.* 2010). Harter (2000) maintains that children with parents who regard their own needs as primary end up with trust and boundary issues in their relationships.

The development of social skills may also be thwarted for children in substance-abusing homes. Children may find it difficult to invite friends over for fear that the parent will be intoxicated/high or because of concern about a parent's erratic moods or sleep patterns; at the same time they may find it difficult to go to others' homes for fear that the parent will not drop them off or pick them up on time, thus thwarting social skills development. Indeed, Eiden *et al.* (2009) found that children of alcoholics had lower social competence than children with nonalcoholic parents. Social incompetence then impairs the ability to relate to others and to interact appropriately.

Human connection and a sense of belonging and acceptance is an important factor for feelings of safety and value. In fact, self-esteem and self-efficacy are developed through supportive relationships (Werner and Johnson 2004).

Best Practices and Treatment Recommendations

Research shows that children of addicted parents who rely on supportive adults show stronger social skills, better coping and increased autonomy (Werner 1986). Indeed, children who recruit parent surrogates and develop strong friendship networks show increased resilience (Wolin and Wolin 1996).

Werner and Johnson (2004) found that children of alcoholics who exhibited fewer problems in adulthood had at least one person in their lives growing up who accepted them unconditionally. And those children who coped *most* effectively relied on an even larger number of social support resources such as grandparents, aunts and uncles, siblings, teachers, ministers, friends, parents of friends, and mental health professionals. The National Association for Children of Alcoholics suggests that counselors and helpers assist children in identifying sympathetic adults who can and do play significant roles in their lives.

Heaney and Israel (2008) suggest the following interventions aimed at enhancing social support:

- **Enhancing existing network ties** refers to changing the attitudes and behaviors of the support recipient (the child) and/or already existing support providers (teachers, ministers, neighbors, etc.).

- **Developing new social network linkages** involves introducing new additional social ties, new to the support recipient (the child). These could include mentors, advisors, "buddies," self-help groups and internet-based support groups.

- **Using indigenous natural helpers and community health workers** requires identifying individuals within a child's own community, who are known for mentoring and providing effective and plentiful support to children in the neighborhood who are troubled or in need. The National Association for Children of Alcoholics (2011) recommends that children create and carry a list of telephone numbers of people who they can call during emergencies.

In addition to social supports, it may be helpful to provide social skills training to children of substance-abusing parents. Social skills training has been proven effective in addressing the needs of multiple at-risk youth populations (August *et al.* 2001; Fraser *et al.* 2000; Lane, Gresham and O'Shaughnessy 2002). Social skills interventions include coaching, modeling, rehearsal, feedback, reinforcement, goal setting, problem solving, discussions and self-evaluation (Maag 2006). Skills include assertiveness, turn taking, conflict resolution, joining in, nonverbal communication, etc. However, it is important to match training with children's individual deficits.

General Suggestions

- Create a trusting relationship with each child.

- Facilitate positive interactions between group members by assisting with problem solving and pointing out similarities between individuals.

- Avoid criticizing inappropriate social skills—instead, teach the preferred skills.

- Draw attention to and compliment prosocial behavior.

- Be alert to discussions among the children regarding potential support systems.

- Encourage children to reach out to safe adults.

- While supporting children's efforts at expanding social networks, also facilitate discussions on how to know if someone is safe (i.e. in relationships with adults, safe adults do not ask children to keep secrets and do not want to always be alone with them; in peer relationships, safe peers want to play together no matter who is around and know how to handle conflict).

Script

"It's really, really important to have supportive people in your life—people you can go to for help, people you can trust, people you can talk to and people who can make you feel good about yourself. Having good people in your life helps you to feel less alone when things aren't going well at home. While your family members are the most important people in your life, it's also nice to have others as well. This requires making sure that they are safe, reaching out to them and practicing good social skills.

During our time together we're going to figure out who the positive people are in your life and the ways that they support you. We're also going to look for ways that you can get *more* positive people in your life. And, finally, we're going to talk about social skills and the ways to act so that your relationships with everyone are good."

Activities

(1) THE COLOURED CANDY GAME

OBJECTIVE

To identify different types of healthy and supportive relationships.

MATERIALS

Fun size packs of colored candy OR a large bag of colored candy, a dry erase board or flip chart and markers.

DIRECTIONS

Prior to the exercise, write the Candy Color Guide on a dry erase board or flip chart. Then give each child a fun size pack of colored candy or, if using a single large bag of candy, give each child 10–15 random candies. Ask children to sort their candy by color and to count how many they have of each color. Then, using the Candy Color Guide, play in one or more of the following ways:

- Using only the candies that children have the most number of, direct them to name one person in their lives in that category.

- Using only the candies that children have the least number of, direct them to name one person in their lives in that category.

- Direct children to close their eyes and select two candies. Upon opening their eyes, have them name two people in their lives that match the color categories they selected.

- Ask children to create a design with their candies. When completed, direct them to take two colors from the center of their designs and to name two people in their lives that match the color categories they selected.

At the end of the game children may eat their candies.

CANDY COLOR GUIDE

RED candies = People who you laugh with.

GREEN candies = People who you feel comfortable and relaxed with.

ORANGE candies = People who you learn a lot of things from.

PURPLE candies = People who you respect and look up to.

YELLOW candies = People who you can talk to about anything.

FOLLOW-UP DISCUSSION QUESTIONS

- Were you happy or disappointed about the types of people you had to name?

- Of the two people that you named, which one was the easiest for you to think of someone? Why?

- Why was your other person more difficult?

- Of the three categories that you didn't have to name, which one do you wish you had got? Why?

- What things did you learn from this activity?

(2) EMERGENCY CALL LIST

OBJECTIVE
To create a list of supportive adults' phone numbers for emergencies.

MATERIALS
Paper and pens or pencils.

DIRECTIONS
Explain to the group that it is always good to have an emergency contact list in case they find themselves in unsafe situations. Give each child a piece of paper and pen or pencil and ask them to write down the names of safe, supportive adults who they could call in the case of an emergency. Then ask them to write down the phone numbers that they know next to the names of the people. For any numbers that they do not know, make a homework assignment of getting them. In order to increase completion of this assignment, offer a reward for numbers returned during the next session. Encourage children to keep their lists in a place where they can easily access them.

FOLLOW-UP DISCUSSION QUESTIONS
- Why did you choose the people that you chose for your list?
- Who would be the first one that you called?
- Where do you think that you will keep your emergency numbers list?
- What kinds of emergencies would cause you to call someone on your list?
- Why is it a good idea to have an emergency list?

(3) CONNECTING GOODNESS AND STRENGTH

OBJECTIVE
To enhance self-esteem and personal connection.

MATERIALS
None.

DIRECTIONS
Explain that it is OK to name good qualities about yourself and others. Describe how when we share similar good qualities it can allow us to feel closer and more connected. Instruct children to break up into pairs and to take a moment to consider their partner's personality and personal characteristics. Then ask each child to identify a positive quality within themselves that they also sense in their partner. Have each one say to the other, "The presence of _____ in me recognizes the presence of _____ in you." Examples might include caring, happiness, silliness, intelligence, strength, etc.

FOLLOW-UP DISCUSSION QUESTIONS

- What was this activity like for you?

- Is it usually difficult for you to accept compliments? Was it a bit easier when your partner acknowledged the same positive quality in her/himself?

- What did you learn about yourself from this exercise?

- What did you learn about your partner?

(4) LISTENING ON PURPOSE

OBJECTIVE

To enhance empathy and good listening skills.

MATERIALS

None.

DIRECTIONS

Explain that all of us really, really like to be heard. In fact, feeling heard causes us to feel special and closer to the person listening to us. However, many times we are thinking more about what *we* are going to say next rather than what the other person is saying. We all need to be better listeners so that we can make others feel special. One way to show that we are listening is to reflect back what we heard the other person say. Have children break up into pairs. Using the topics below (or others that might seem appropriate) ask each child to take one minute to talk about a topic. Then have the partner reflect on what she/he heard. Hint: a good reflection starts out with the word "You." Possible topics are:

- a conflict you had with a family member

- a fun time at recess

- a hobby

- an embarrassing moment

- a happy holiday

- a difficult holiday

- a time you were worried about a parent.

FOLLOW-UP DISCUSSION QUESTIONS

- What was this activity like for you?

- Was it difficult to talk for one whole minute? Was it difficult to listen for one whole minute?

- How did it feel when your partner reflected back to you what you had talked about?

- When could you use reflective listening in your life outside of this group?

(5) GOLD MEDAL COMPLIMENTS

OBJECTIVE
To increase prosocial behavior and build cohesion in the group.

MATERIALS
Cardboard circles, ribbon, markers, glitter and glue.

DIRECTIONS
Ask the group to make some positive compliments people like to hear. (Encourage children to come up with things that are specific and not based on looks or appearance—e.g. smart, funny, strong, good at dancing, etc.) Then, ask each one to look at the person on their right and come up with a compliment for that person. Next, have them decorate a cardboard "medal" using the idea of the compliment. Once the medals are finished, invite each child to present the medal and tell what it is for.

FOLLOW-UP DISCUSSION QUESTIONS

- What does it feel like to receive a compliment?

- What does it feel like to give a compliment?

- Why should people give each other compliments?

- Is there anyone outside of this group who you would like to give a compliment to? How and when would you do it?

Worksheet Discussion Questions

How People Help Me lists various ways in which people are supportive or helpful. It asks children to list the names of people who are important to them and then to draw lines from each name to the ways in which that person is supportive. After completing the worksheet, the following discussion questions can be used:

- How many of the people you listed are helpful to you in more than one way?

- Of all the different ways that people can be helpful or supportive, which type of support do you get the most of?

- Which type of support do you wish you had more of?

- Can you think of people you would like to add to this list in the future? Who are they?

People I Trust recognizes some of the different types of trust. It asks children to identify people in their lives who they can trust in various ways and to draw pictures of them. After completing the worksheet, the following discussion questions can be used:

- What is trust?

- Who are some of the people you can trust? How does it feel to be able to trust others?

- If you trust someone, do you have to be able to trust her/him for everything or can you trust different people for different things?

- Can other people trust *you*? What kinds of things can they trust you for?

Expanding My Support Network invites children to think about positive adults and peers who they could invite into their lives. It challenges them to select three of these people and come up with a plan for getting to know them better. After completing the worksheet, the following discussion questions can be used:

- Who are some of the people you would like to get to know better?

- What is your plan to get to know them better? If that plan doesn't work, do you have another plan that you can use?

- How scary is it to get to know new people? How do you calm down your scared feelings?

- Of the three people you wrote down, which one do you think you'll try to get to know first?

Rating My Social Skills lists ten important social skills necessary for children to make and keep friends. It asks children to rank their competence in each area. After completing the worksheet, the following discussion questions can be used:

- Which social skill do you think you are best at? What social skill would *others* say is your strongest?

- Which social skill do you need to work on?

- How would you work on this? What would be your plan?

- Why are social skills important?

Boundaries, Boundaries, Boundaries describes different kinds of boundaries (physical space boundaries, material boundaries and emotional boundaries) and asks children to differentiate a list of behaviors as good boundaries or boundary violations. After completing the worksheet, the following discussion questions can be used:

- Have you ever had any of the boundary problems listed on the worksheet?

- What are some of your most important boundaries?

- How does it feel when someone violates your boundaries?

- Do others respect your boundaries? Who does and who does not?

How People Help Me

Using the lines to the left, write down the names of the important people in your life. They can be friends, relatives, teachers, ministers, parents of friends, etc. You don't have to fill all the lines but fill as many as you can. Then draw lines from each name to the ways in which that person is helpful or supportive of you. You can draw as many lines as you like.

_____

_____

_____

_____

_____

_____

_____

_____

_____

Spends time with me

Treats me fairly

Listens to me

Makes me laugh

Sticks up for me

Makes or gives me snacks

Answers my questions

Accepts me just the way I am

Helps me with schoolwork

Encourages me

People I Trust

There are many ways to trust people. Think about each of the ways listed below. Then write a person's name in each of the blank spaces who fits that description and draw a picture of her/him. You can use the same name more than once but try to think of as many different people as you can.

I trust _____ to be honest with me even when it's hard.

I trust _____ to remain calm in upsetting situations.

I trust _____ to admit her/ his own mistakes when she/he makes them.

I trust _____ to forgive me when I make mistakes.

Expanding My Support Network

Even though you care about the people already in your life, it's always good to have additional safe and supportive folks around you. Think about some of the people who you don't know very well but would like to get to know better—teachers, coaches, neighbors, classmates, church members, friends' parents, etc. Write down three names of people you would like to get to know better and then answer the questions.

Name of person _____

What do you like about her/him?_____

How do you know she/he is a safe person? _____

What is your plan to try to get to know her/him better (examples: go up and talk to her/him; ask someone to introduce you; hang out where she/he hangs out; etc.)? _____

Name of person _____

What do you like about her/him?_____

How do you know she/he is a safe person? _____

What is your plan to try to get to know her/him better (examples: go up and talk to her/him; ask someone to introduce you; hang out where she/he hangs out; etc.)? _____

Name of person _____

What do you like about her/him?_____

How do you know she/he is a safe person? _____

What is your plan to try to get to know her/him better (examples: go up and talk to her/him; ask someone to introduce you; hang out where she/he hangs out; etc.)? _____

Rating My Social Skills

In order to make and keep friends it is important to *be* a good friend. This requires social skills. Look at the specific social skills listed below and give yourself a 1–5 star rating (1 = very low; 2 = sort of low; 3 = medium; 4 = high; 5 = very high) on each item by coloring in the number of stars that you think shows your level. Remember, *all* of us have strengths and weaknesses.

I share my toys and belongings.	☆ ☆ ☆ ☆ ☆
I give other kids compliments.	☆ ☆ ☆ ☆ ☆
I stop myself from being bossy.	☆ ☆ ☆ ☆ ☆
I settle disagreements in a friendly way.	☆ ☆ ☆ ☆ ☆
I *ask* to join in instead of jumping in.	☆ ☆ ☆ ☆ ☆
I show an interest in others' interests.	☆ ☆ ☆ ☆ ☆
I can read others' body language.	☆ ☆ ☆ ☆ ☆
I listen when others talk.	☆ ☆ ☆ ☆ ☆
I smile at others when I pass them.	☆ ☆ ☆ ☆ ☆
I offer to help others when they need it.	☆ ☆ ☆ ☆ ☆

Boundaries, Boundaries, Boundaries

Boundaries are the rules or limits that you set in order to feel safe with others. There are **physical space boundaries** (how close you want others to get to you); **material boundaries** (who you allow to touch or borrow your things); and **emotional boundaries** (keeping your emotions separate from others' emotions). Listed on the left side of the page are different behaviors. Read each one and decide if it describes a good boundary or a boundary violation. Then draw a line from the behavior to the smiley face if it describes a good boundary and draw a line from the behavior to the sad face if it describes a boundary violation.

Letting other kids boss you around.

Pushing others to get out of your way.

Saying "No" to friends who want you to do something you are uncomfortable with.

Borrowing someone's book without asking.

Asking someone permission before giving her/him a hug.

Telling someone what she/he should do.

Standing back while someone gets a drink at the drinking fountain.

Making sure that your lunch stays in the space in front of you on the table.

Jumping into a game that has already started.

Agreeing to disagree when a friend has a different opinion from you.

CHAPTER 7

Improving Impulse Control

Introduction

Impulsivity is defined as a predisposition toward rapid, unplanned reactions and behaviors without thought to possible consequences of those actions. It can include components of sensation seeking, lack of forethought, aggressiveness, and poor problem solving. It is the personality trait most associated with being a child of an alcoholic (Sher 1997; Sher *et al.* 1991). Several studies have found that children of alcoholics are more hyperactive and impulsive than other children (e.g. Bell and Cohen 1981; Knop *et al.* 1985). Other studies have found that those children of alcoholics who had active, excitable and risk-taking temperaments developed serious coping problems in their teens (Mylant *et al.* 2002).

Childhood impulsivity contributes to social maladjustment which is a risk factor for substance abuse (Tarter *et al.* 2004). In addition, impulsivity is associated with early substance experimentation and with substance abuse disorders, making impulsivity both a risk factor for and a consequence of substance abuse (Dom *et al.* 2006; Moeller and Dougherty 2002). Tarter *et al.* (2003) found that at age 16, impulsivity is a stronger predictor of substance abuse disorders than substance use frequency. Sher and Trull (1994) acknowledged that impulsivity may be a major component in the development of alcoholism and may be an important factor in the intergenerational transmission of alcoholism.

In the classic marshmallow experiment several decades ago, marshmallows were offered to four-year-olds. They were told that they could eat one marshmallow immediately or, if they could wait until the examiner left and returned, they could have two marshmallows. Some children ate their marshmallow immediately (the "grabbers"); some delayed eating (the "waiters").

Fourteen years later, significant differences were discovered between the "grabbers" and the "waiters." The "grabbers" were easily frustrated, had greater relationship problems and had lower self-esteem. The "waiters" were more flexible and socially competent; they had higher self-esteem; their grades were higher; and, even while controlling for IQ, had SAT scores that were 210 points higher. Further research has confirmed that children who lack impulse control are at risk for relationship problems, inferior academics, behavior problems, substance abuse problems and poor self-perceptions (Mischel and Ebbesen 1970).

Best Practices and Treatment Recommendations

Self-talk is a regulatory strategy and impulsive individuals do not make good use of internalized talk. Tullet and Inzlicht (2010) found that subjects acted more impulsively (and less efficiently) when they couldn't verbalize messages to themselves during a task. Self-instruction (or teaching self-talk) is effective in reducing impulsivity/hyperactivity and increasing reflectivity and academic performance (Gargallo 1993; Meftagh *et al.* 2011). Miranda *et al.* (2011) also found that self-instruction along with teaching problem-solving skills improved impulsive children's planning, task analysis and problem solving.

In addition to self-instruction, studies show that imposing a forced delay on impulsive children also increases accuracy in schoolwork (Gargallo 1993; Maggiore 1983). The purpose of a forced delay is to slow down responses and avoid hasty behaviors. Encouraging thoughtful responding by waiting five to ten seconds enhances reflectivity, the contrast to impulsivity.

Dialectical Behavioral Therapy (DBT) is a treatment that was originally developed for borderline personality disorder (BPD) with the goals of minimizing maladaptive behaviors due to impulsivity and poor emotion regulation. Research has also found that DBT techniques also decrease impulsivity among behaviorally disordered youth (Marco, Garcia-Palacios and Botella 2013; Quinn and Shera 2009; Shelton *et al.* 2011; Zylowska *et al.* 2008). DBT focuses on helping clients "accept" uncomfortable thoughts and feelings using mindfulness and relaxation. Using these techniques, individuals develop the ability to accept distressing thoughts and to tolerate self-destructive urges without acting upon them. In a related study, elementary aged students who participated in a mindful awareness practices program had improvements in behavioral regulation and executive functioning (Flook *et al.* 2010).

General Suggestions

- Compliment children on displays/practices of impulse *control* when they happen in the moment.

- If you see a child about to engage in an impulsive behavior, stop and ask her/ him what might happen (consequences) if she/he went ahead and did it.

- Model reflectivity by thinking *out loud.*

- If conflicts or problems pop up during group sessions, identify the problem ("It looks like both of you want the same chair," "All of you want to go first in the game," etc.) and then ask the children to come up with three solutions for it (stop and think!).

- Allow times for children to share their impulse control successes of the week using the template: "I had the impulse to _____, but I stopped and thought _____, and decided to do _____ instead."

Script

"An impulse is a feeling or urge to do something quickly. All of us have impulses. We have impulses to yell at people, to hug people, to borrow something without asking, etc. The question is: are you the boss of your impulses or are your impulses the boss of you? If you let your impulses be the boss of you, you don't plan or think about what you're doing—and that probably gets you into trouble!

If you're the boss of your impulses, you stop yourself and think: 'Is this impulse a good choice or a bad choice?' You decide if it's a good choice or a bad choice by thinking about the consequences— 'What will happen next if I act on this impulse?' For example, if you have the impulse to shout out the answer to the teacher's question without raising your hand, you can stop yourself and think about how that might get you into trouble and then decide to raise your hand instead. Let's get ready for this lesson by saying out loud, 'Stop and think; stop and think; stop and think.'" (NOTE: have children say this over and over again like a refrain.)

Activities

(1) THE IMPULSE CONTROL CANDYLAND® GAME

OBJECTIVE

To consider consequences, identify personal impulse control successes and practice control.

MATERIALS

CandyLand® game* and Appendices C and D.

DIRECTIONS

Explain that learning how to improve impulse control involves slowing down to think. In this game players will have opportunities to slow down to think about the consequences of certain impulses and to identify what self-talk they used for their own personal impulse control successes. Using the CandyLand® game board and pieces, players will take turns moving around the board according to the CandyLand® game directions. However, when landing on the various colors players will follow the directions below:

- If players land on *red* or *purple* spaces, they will describe what the consequences (outcomes) might be if they gave in to specific impulses. A list of impulses can

---

* Other colored game boards can be substituted for CandyLand® but modifications will need to be made for the colors in the instructions.

be found in Appendix C. Players or the group facilitator will read a different impulse for each turn on a *red* or *purple* space.

- If players land on *yellow* or *blue* spaces, they will describe one of their own personal impulse control successes by using the phrase "I once had the impulse to _____ but I stopped and thought _____ and did _____ instead."

- If players land on *brown* or *green* spaces, they will select one of the behaviors listed on Appendix D to perform continuously until the person on their right says "Stop!" If players stop immediately on command they go forward two spaces. If players are not able to stop on command, they must go back two spaces. When landing on a new color (either forward or back) on this turn players do not have to perform the new color task.

If players do not wish to answer a particular question they can PASS but will have to go back to their original space (this would be like skipping a turn).

FOLLOW-UP DISCUSSION QUESTIONS

- Everyone has impulses. Do you think that you are the boss of your impulses or are your impulses the boss of you?

- The secret to impulse control is to stop and think before acting. What are some ways you can get yourself to stop before you decide what to do in a situation?

- In what ways will improving your impulse control help you?

(2) IT'S OK TO TALK TO MYSELF

OBJECTIVE
To increase internalized speech or self-talk.

MATERIALS
Jenga® or a different tumbling blocks game.

DIRECTIONS
Explain again that sometimes it's good to talk to ourselves. It helps to think about what we're doing and make better decisions. Using a Jenga® game or another type of tumbling blocks game, instruct children to analyze the tower as they play and to "think out loud" when it is their turn. As the object of the game is to remove blocks from the tower without causing it to fall, children might think out loud with statements such as "The tower looks like it's leaning a bit to the left so I think I'll pull a block out of the right side so it doesn't fall over" or "This block feels pretty tight in the stack; I'd better find a looser one." Play until the tower falls.

FOLLOW-UP DISCUSSION QUESTIONS

- Did thinking out loud help you make better plays in your games?

- How does thinking before acting help you in real life?

- How could you teach yourself to think more before acting?

- What did you learn about yourself in this game?

(3) MINDFULLY BREATHING

OBJECTIVE

To develop calming and focusing skills.

MATERIALS

None.

DIRECTIONS

Explain that mindful breathing is a way to get quiet, calm and focused (the opposite of impulsive!). It trains your mind to slow down, relax and think clearly. Instruct students to close their eyes (if they wish) and think about their breathing. Walk them through mindful breathing with a script similar to the following:

As you breathe in, think about the air coming up through your nose, your lungs filling up with air, and your ribs swelling. As you exhale, think about the air leaving through your nose, your lungs shrinking and ribs lying back to rest. If your mind starts to wander off to something else, calmly say to yourself "breathing" and turn your attention back to your breath.

Instruct the children to continue this for three to five minutes.

FOLLOW-UP DISCUSSION QUESTIONS

- How hard was it to stay focused?

- How do you feel now after doing this exercise?

- When do you think you could use this exercise in your real life?

- What did you learn about yourself during this exercise?

(4) SIMON SAYS

OBJECTIVE

To improve thinking before acting.

MATERIALS

None.

DIRECTIONS

Explain that having good impulse control means thinking before acting and that the game *Simon Says* requires them to do just that. *Simon Says* is a child's game for two or more players where a facilitator (or third player) takes the role of "Simon" and delivers commands (e.g. "hop up and down," "take one step forward," "wave your right arm," etc.) to the players. Commands should *only* be followed if prefaced with the phrase "Simon says." For example, "Simon says, hop up and down." In the original game, players are eliminated from the game when they follow instructions that are not preceded by the phrase, "Simon says" or by failing to follow an instruction which includes the phrase "Simon says." In our version, players receive points for following directives preceded by "Simon says" or refraining from following directives which are not preceded by "Simon says." The object of the game is to distinguish between valid and invalid commands—not physical ability.

FOLLOW-UP DISCUSSION QUESTIONS

- How hard was it to listen for the phrase "Simon says?"
- What did you have to do to be successful at the game?
- What did you have to tell yourself?
- How are the skills that you learned in this game something that you can use in real life?

(5) TO EAT OR NOT TO EAT: THAT IS THE QUESTION

OBJECTIVE

To improve delayed gratification.

MATERIALS

Candy.

DIRECTIONS

Explain that learning how to wait for things is essential for reaching goals and experiencing success in life. Then place a piece of candy in front of each child and tell them that they can either eat that piece now or wait three to five minutes (depending on the ages of the children in the group) and receive three pieces of candy. Wait the allotted time and then reward those who waited. (Generally, all of the children wait because of peer pressure from the group.)

FOLLOW-UP DISCUSSION QUESTIONS

- How hard was it to wait? Were you tempted to eat the first piece of candy?
- How did you stop yourself from eating the first piece of candy?

- What are some other ways you have put off immediate pleasure for something better in the future?

- Why do you think it's important to learn how to put off immediate pleasure?

Worksheet Discussion Questions

Impulse Control Report Card asks children to evaluate their impulse control by "grading" various behaviors that require restraint or reflectivity. It then asks them to develop a plan for a weak area. After completing the worksheet, the following discussion questions can be used:

- As you did this worksheet, did you stop and think about each item before giving yourself a grade on it or did you just quickly answer each item?

- Which item on the report card were you the strongest in? Which one were you the weakest in?

- What is your plan to improve your weak area?

- Can you think of any other behaviors that could have been listed on this report card?

Slow Down and Think about Consequences lists five situations where a child has an impulse to behave in a manner that potentially could have a negative outcome. Five possible consequences are also listed. The directions are to match the impulse with the consequence. After completing the worksheet, the following discussion questions can be used:

- Do all actions have consequences? Do positive behaviors have positive consequences? Give an example.

- Have you ever experienced any negative consequences for impulsive behavior?

- Have you ever experienced any positive consequences for good behavior?

- When is a time that you have had an impulse to do something but stopped yourself by thinking about the consequences?

Talk to Yourself presents five situations where someone might react impulsively. It asks children to write down what they could tell themselves in order to resist the impulse. After completing the worksheet, the following discussion questions can be used:

- Have you ever had any of the impulses listed on this worksheet? How did it work out?

- What are some other impulses that you frequently have? What could you tell yourself about those?

- Why is it good to talk to yourself before acting?

- What are some ways that you could remind yourself to slow down and think before acting?

Think It or Say It? presents several statements that kids make and asks children to differentiate those things that are OK to be said out loud and those things that are better left as thoughts, and unsaid. After completing the worksheet, the following discussion questions can be used:

- Why shouldn't people simply blurt out everything that pops into their heads?

- Have you ever said something that you later regretted?

- Look at the statements on the worksheet that you decided shouldn't be said out loud. What is wrong with each of them? What might happen?

- How can you remind yourself to think before speaking?

My Impulse Control Successes asks children to complete three sentences that identify times when they successfully used impulse control—in the classroom, on the playground and at home. After completing the worksheet, the following discussion questions can be used:

- What do you think about the fact that you were able to identify times when you used good impulse control? How does it feel?

- Why do you think you were successful in those situations? What skills did you use?

- What do you think it says about you as a person that you were able to control your impulses?

- What did you learn from doing this worksheet? What things did you use in these situations that you could use again?

Impulse Control Report Card

Impulse control affects many different behaviors. Look at the behaviors below and give yourself a "grade" for each one. Then respond to the questions at the bottom of the page.

I stop myself from interrupting others.	
I control my anger.	
I raise my hand in class and wait to be called on when I want to say or ask something.	
I think of several solutions to a problem before I do anything.	
I wait patiently when I am in line for something.	
I am a good listener.	
I think about the consequences when I get an urge to do something.	

Which impulse control skill are you best at? _____

_____

Which impulse control skill do you need the most work on? _____

_____

What is your plan to work on it?_____

_____

_____

Slow Down and Think about Consequences

On the left side of the page are some impulses or urges that lots of children experience. On the right side of the page are possible consequences. Think about each situation and draw a line from the impulse to the possible consequence.

You have the impulse to yell at your parent when you see she/he is drunk/high.

Your neighbor might feel quite upset and tell your parent what you did.

You have the impulse to pick some flowers for your mom out of your neighbor's yard.

Your sibling might become angry with you.

You have the impulse to argue with your parent when she/he says you can't go outside.

Your teacher might give you a punishment or lecture you in front of the class.

You have the impulse to talk to your classmate while the teacher is talking.

Your parent might become physically or verbally aggressive with you.

You have the impulse to change the TV channel while your sibling is watching her/his show.

Your parent might ground you from something you enjoy.

Talk to Yourself

Listed below are some impulses that children often experience. If you slowed down and talked to yourself, what would you tell yourself in each of the following situations in order to resist the impulse? Write down your answer.

It's very quiet in the classroom and you have the impulse to burp loudly on purpose. What should you tell yourself? _____

_____

Your parent fell asleep on the couch with a large bottle of liquor in front of her/him and you have the impulse to pour it out. What should you tell yourself? _____

_____

A classmate is making fun of your parent's substance abuse problem and you have the impulse to tell her/him to shut up. What should you tell yourself? _____

_____

Your teacher just yelled at you and you have the impulse to yell back at her. What should you tell yourself? _____

_____

You're putting your shirt on and it gets twisted. You are feeling frustrated and have the impulse to rip it. What should you tell yourself? _____

_____

Think It or Say It?

It is not a good idea to say everything that pops into your head. Some things are better left unsaid and left as thoughts rather than turned into speech. Look at the statements below and, if they are OK to say, draw lines from them to the speech bubble. If they are not OK to say, draw lines from them to the thought bubble.

 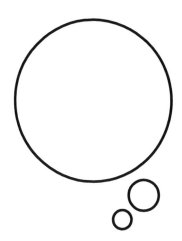

"You're a good soccer player!"

"That's a stupid idea."

"You're old! Are you going to die soon?"

"I think I messed up. Sorry!"

"I'd like some salt please."

"Ewwww, you need to brush your teeth."

"He likes mustard on his hamburgers."

"Your breath smells like rotten onions."

"Please stop doing that."

"Man, that outfit looks ridiculous!"

"What time should I come over on Saturday?"

"Your haircut makes you look like a skunk."

"Your pants are too tight. I can see your flab."

"You're funny!"

My Impulse Control Successes

Even if you think you have trouble controlling your impulses, there are still times when you really have controlled them. Write down those successes in the spaces below.

In the classroom I had the impulse to _____

but I stopped myself and thought_____

and did_____ instead.

On the playground I had the impulse to _____

but I stopped myself and thought_____

and did _____ instead.

At home I had the impulse to _____

but I stopped myself and thought_____

and did_____ instead.

CHAPTER 8

Problem Solving and Goal Setting

Introduction

Billings *et al.* (1979) found that impaired problem-solving abilities are observable in highly problematic families, including families where there is substance abuse. Other studies have specifically shown how alcoholic families demonstrate poorer problem-solving abilities than non-alcoholic families (Sher 1997). Children from these families consequently "inherit" these problem-solving deficits (Mylant *et al.* 2002).

Research suggests that children who lack crucial problem-solving skills are often behaviorally challenging or difficult (Greene *et al.* 2002). Each difficult child has a "pile" of unsolved problems that consistently cause challenging behavior. In addition, poor problem-solving skills have been associated with depression, anxiety and antisocial behaviors (Kazdin, Siegel and Bass 1992; Siu and Shek 2010).

A study of women with and without substance-abusing parents found that those with substance-abusing parents used avoidant coping more than approach coping (Amodeo *et al.* 2007). *Avoidant coping* involves denying, minimizing or attempting to escape stressful situations, whereas *approach coping* involves efforts to master or resolve problems (Moos 1992). Approach coping, including problem solving, is associated with more self-confidence and fewer social/emotional problems (Moos 2002).

Effective problem solving is indeed an important coping strategy, decreasing stress and negative affect. Children's problem-solving skills are an important part of overall social competence. Problem solving allows children to stay calm during difficult situations, attend to conflicts more productively, and get their needs met in ways that are safe and fair.

In addition, goal setting is an important element for self-regulation and performance (Schunk 1990). Locke and Latham (2002) suggest that goal setting focuses attention toward goal-relevant activities (and away from unrelated activities), energizes, enhances persistence and activates coping strategies—all relevant and important qualities needed for children of substance-abusing parents in order to enhance resiliency.

Best Practices and Treatment Recommendations

Most programs for children of substance-abusing parents teach general problem-solving skills and/or specific problem-focused coping skills (Cuijpers 2005; Nastasi and DeZolt 1994). These groups typically teach children how to generate alternative solutions and manage interpersonal conflicts using modeling, role playing and corrective feedback.

Problem-solving skills training has been highly effective in reducing depression, aggression and delinquent behaviors among behaviorally disordered children (Becker-Weidman *et al.* 2010; Greene *et al.* 2004; Kazdin *et al.* 1992). Problem-solving programs have also been shown to increase children's emotional intelligence and prosocial skills (Hassan and Mouganie 2014). In studying resiliency in high-risk environments, Werner and Smith (1992) found that resilient persons have good problem-solving skills and a sense of purpose and future.

Creating a sense of purpose and future involves goal setting—a task that enhances mastery, coping skills, self-motivation and self-direction. Stein *et al.* (1997) found that the creation of clearly defined goals was predictive of adaptive coping. Tangible goal achievement ameliorates feelings of anxiety, futility and a lack of control (Bandura 1982).

While there are no studies regarding goal setting among children of substance-abusing parents, a study with learning disabled students showed students with goals (either self-set or teacher-set) exhibited greater self-regulated learning than students with no goals. It was also found that students with self-set goals produced greater self-efficacy and task performance than students with teacher-set goals (Schunk 1985).

General Suggestions

- Model good problem-solving skills by thinking out loud of alternate solutions when facing a challenge during the group.

- As various problems arise among the children in the group (e.g. two children want to sit in the same chair, everyone wants to go first in a game, etc.), stop and identify the problem and ask the children to come up with three solutions.

- Post inspirational quotations around the room that enhance motivation for goal setting and problem solving. Here are some examples but post as many as you can find:

  ◦ "Do it, and then you will feel motivated to do it." (Zig Ziglar)

  ◦ "The secret of getting ahead is getting started." (Mark Twain)

  ◦ "Everything you want is out there waiting for you to ask. Everything you want also wants you. But you have to take action to get it." (Jules Renau)

  ◦ "I never worry about action, but only about inaction." (Winston Churchill)

- ◦ "I don't say: 'can't do that,' 'won't do that.' I've never thought in that way about work." (Daniel Craig)

- ◦ "Respect your efforts, respect yourself. Self-respect leads to self-discipline. When you have both firmly under your belt, that's real power." (Clint Eastwood)

- ◦ "A lot of people give up just before they're about to make it. You know you never know when that next obstacle is going to be the last one." (Chuck Norris)

- ◦ "It's not whether you get knocked down, it's whether you get up." (Vince Lombardi)

- ◦ "I've failed over and over and over again in my life and that is why I succeed." (Michael Jordan)

- ◦ "It's hard to beat a person who never gives up." (Babe Ruth)

Script

"Everyone encounters problems. It's just part of being human. Being a good problem *solver*, though, means that for every problem you can name, you can think of several solutions for it. You're not stuck on just the first solution that pops into your head. And, when you think about those solutions, you can decide which one is the best choice by thinking about the pros and cons of each one. That's when you're ready to pick the best one and do it! Bingo! Great problem solver!

We're also going to talk about goal setting. Setting goals for yourself gives you a path to follow—a positive direction to go in. It helps you plan the actions you need to do in order to get where you want to go. It puts YOU in the 'driver's seat' of your life.

Being a good problem solver and setting goals for yourself will really make you feel good about yourself! And that's FABULOUS!"

Activities

(1) PUTTING THE PIECES TOGETHER

OBJECTIVE
To practice problem-solving skills and co-operation.

MATERIALS
Several eight- to ten-piece children's jigsaw puzzles.

DIRECTIONS

Explain that, ordinarily when children play with puzzles, they get to look at the picture to guide them in putting the pieces together. In this activity there will be no picture because the puzzle will be turned upside down. Have children sit in small groups of two or three; give each group a set of puzzle pieces turned upside down. Explain that good problem solving involves coming up with several solutions before picking one to try. Ask children for several ideas regarding how to solve the problem of putting the puzzle together without a picture. Then allow each group to decide which strategy they would like to try first and have them attempt to put the puzzle together. Some will be successful and others will not. If unsuccessful groups appear frustrated ask them what other solutions they would like to try.

FOLLOW-UP DISCUSSION QUESTIONS

- How hard was it to put the puzzle together without a picture? Did you feel frustrated?

- How many ideas did you come up with to solve the problem? Which solution worked? Was it the first solution that you thought of?

- How well did your group co-operate while you were trying to put the puzzle together?

- Are there some problems in life that really do require asking others for assistance?

(2) PROBLEM-SOLVING BALL TOSS

OBJECTIVE

To enhance solution-generating skills.

MATERIALS

Medium-size ball.

DIRECTIONS

Explain that whenever a problem arises, there are always multiple solutions to it. Some solutions may be better than others but there are always several answers. Instruct children to stand in a circle facing one another. Hand a ball to one of the children in the circle and ask her/him to think of a problem (any problem will do—real or hypothetical, school-related or home-related, etc.). Have her/him state the problem, then call out one of the other children's name and toss the ball to her/him. The "catcher" must state a potential solution to the problem, call out another child's name and throw the ball to her/him. The next child will state another solution, call out another child's name and throw the ball to her/him. This child will state a third solution to the original problem, call out another child's name and throw the ball to her/him. After three solutions are generated, the next child to receive the ball will state another question and follow the directions above. The game should continue until at least five problems have been addressed but it is up to the counselor's discretion.

FOLLOW-UP DISCUSSION QUESTIONS

- How hard was it to come up with three solutions for every problem?
- Why do you think it's a good idea to think of several solutions before trying one?
- How would your life be different if you took time to think of multiple solutions before trying to address a problem?
- Who do you know who you think is a good problem solver? Why?

(3) EVALUATING THE PROS AND CONS

OBJECTIVE
To practice evaluating potential solutions to problems.

MATERIALS
Colored index cards and pens or pencils.

DIRECTIONS
Prior to the activity take out four cards of each color. On *one* of *each* of the different colored cards write down a problem and on the other three cards of the *same* color write down three different solutions to that problem. Do this with each color. Keep the problem cards. Shuffle the solution cards and then "deal" the solution cards out to the children. Explain to the children that after identifying a problem and thinking of several solutions, it is helpful to examine the pros and cons of each solution. Explain that you will read a problem card in a particular color. Every person holding the same color card will read off the solution that is written on the card and then name one good thing (a "pro") and one bad thing (a "con") to their solution. Feel free to come up with your own problems and solutions but here are some examples:

PROBLEM CARD: Your parent is passed out on the couch and you need her/him to take you to school.

SOLUTION CARD 1: Skip school that day.

SOLUTION CARD 2: Try to wake up your parent.

SOLUTION CARD 3: Call someone else to take you.

PROBLEM CARD: There are a couple of kids in your class who make fun of you for being late to school so much.

SOLUTION CARD 1: Ignore them.

SOLUTION CARD 2: Tell the teacher on them.

SOLUTION CARD 3: Start a conversation with them about something else.

PROBLEM CARD: You see your best friend cheating on a math test.

SOLUTION CARD 1: Pretend you didn't see.

SOLUTION CARD 2: Tell the teacher on her/him.

SOLUTION CARD 3: Tell your friend that you saw her/him cheating.

FOLLOW-UP DISCUSSION QUESTIONS

- Do you think that examining the pros and cons of a solution would be helpful in making good choices? Why?

- Have you ever taken the time to think about the pros and cons to a particular solution? What happened?

- Some people like to write a pros and cons list. Would you ever do that? Would it make any difference for you to see your pros and cons in writing?

- How do you feel about yourself when you make good choices about the problems you face?

(4) ACTION STEPS

OBJECTIVE
To learn how to organize an action plan for a specific goal.

MATERIALS
Poster boards and markers.

DIRECTIONS
Explain to the group that having goals is wonderful but, in order to reach those goals, it's important to identify the steps needed in reaching that goal. Ask them to draw a large staircase with a picture of one of their goals at the top of the stairs. Then direct them to write down specific action steps that they need to take in order to achieve the goal on the individual steps. For example, if one of the goals is to go to college, some of the steps might be to get help in math, do homework, study for tests, get college applications, take college entrance exams, etc.

FOLLOW-UP DISCUSSION QUESTIONS

- How many "steps" do you have for reaching your goal?
- Which step will be the easiest? The hardest?
- What will you need to make it past the hardest step?
- What obstacles might you encounter as you head towards your goal? How will you overcome them?

(5) OVERCOMING OBSTACLES

OBJECTIVE
To recognize that obstacles to goals can be overcome.

MATERIALS
Three or four orange colored poster boards, tape, paper and pens.

DIRECTIONS
Prior to meeting with the group, twist and tape several orange poster boards into cone shapes to look like roadside safety cones. Then place two strands of tape parallel to one another on the floor to create a "road." Put the "safety cones" at various places on the "road" and a chair at the end of the "road." Explain to the group that when people wish to arrive at one of their goals, they often have to travel down a "road" to get there—and that there are often obstacles along the way. Then direct children to write down one of their goals on a piece of paper. (Any kind of goal is fine—athletic, educational, relationship, etc.) One at a time, have each child:

1. Place her/his written goal on the chair.

2. Place her/himself at the opposite end of the "road."

3. Walk down the "road" towards the goal and, when meeting an obstacle (a "safety cone"), stop and state what one of the obstacles might be in achieving her/his goal along with two possible ways that obstacle might be overcome. (If children have difficulty thinking of obstacles or solutions to obstacles, they can ask the group for assistance.)

4. Move the obstacle out of the "road" and continue to the next obstacle.

5. Repeat the naming of an obstacle and two possible solutions until all obstacles are gone and she/he can "rest" on the chair, holding up the written goal in a gesture of triumph.

FOLLOW-UP DISCUSSION QUESTIONS

- Do you think that all goals have obstacles? Should obstacles stop you from reaching your goals?

- When you hit obstacles to your goals, do you have to handle them by yourself? Who can you ask for assistance?

- Can you think of a famous person who accomplished one of her/his goals? Do you think she/he had any obstacles along the way? What might some of them have been?

- What do you like about having goals?

Worksheet Discussion Questions

Brainstorming identifies a typical problem for many students and asks children to brainstorm multiple solutions to the problem. After completing the worksheet, the following discussion questions can be used:

- Were you able to think of five solutions? If not, how many did you think of?

- Have you ever brainstormed ideas before? What was it for? How did it work out?

- Why is it better to brainstorm solutions to a problem rather than simply act on the first solution that comes to mind?

- What are some problems in your life that brainstorming would help with?

Problem Solving asks children to identify a real-life problem that they are struggling with. It then directs them to generate three solutions, examine the pros and cons of each solution and select the best one. After completing the worksheet, the following discussion questions can be used:

- What kinds of problems do you encounter at home? At school?

- How do you typically handle these problems?

- What makes a good problem solver? What qualities do you think that they have?

- Do you feel better about a solution to your problem on this worksheet? How will you know if your solution worked?

Fact Finding explains how important it is to gather information before making decisions. It presents three scenarios and asks children what additional information they need and where they can get that information. After completing the worksheet, the following discussion questions can be used:

- Gathering information can help keep you from jumping to conclusions or assuming things wrongly. What does it mean to jump to conclusions or assume?

- Have you ever made a bad decision because you assumed instead of getting the facts? What happened?

- Where are the best places to go to get the facts?

- What do you need to tell yourself in order to stay calm while you are gathering facts?

Values and Goals asks children to identify five of their most important values (values words are listed in Appendix E) and then to create a goal for each one. After completing the worksheet, the following discussion questions can be used:

- What are some of your values? Where do you think these came from?

- Do all of you in this group have the same values? Is it OK to have different values?

- Which values do you share with your family members and which values do you have that are different from them?

- What are some of your goals related to your values? Why is it important to have goals that fit your values?

Goals, Goals, Goals directs children to think about goals that they have for different areas of their lives; areas include education, family, friends, behavior, body/physical well-being and fun. After completing the worksheet, the following discussion questions can be used:

- Why is it important to set goals for yourself?

- What are some of your goals?

- What is the difference between goals and dreams?

- What are some goals that you have already accomplished? How were you able to accomplish them?

Brainstorming

In order to be a good problem solver, it is helpful to think of as many solutions as possible before deciding on one to try. In the center circle below there is a problem that many kids have at school. In the outer circles write down as many solutions for the problem as you can think of.

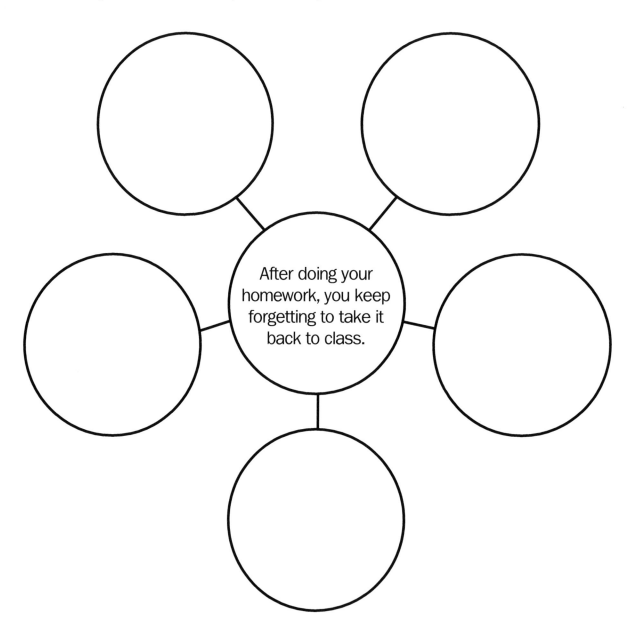

After doing your homework, you keep forgetting to take it back to class.

Problem Solving

Solve a problem you have been struggling with by writing the problem in the first box and then following the steps of identifying solutions, examining the pros and cons of each solution and selecting the best solution.

Identify the problem

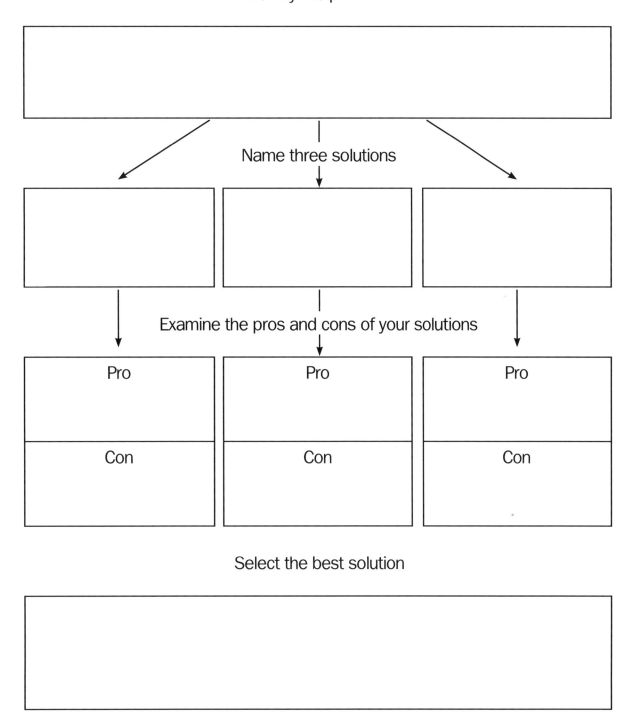

Name three solutions

Examine the pros and cons of your solutions

Pro	Pro	Pro
Con	Con	Con

Select the best solution

Fact Finding

When problems arise it's useful to gather as much information as possible to help in decision making. Listed below are several problems. Read them and then write down what additional information you might need in order to come up with the best possible solution.

You heard from someone in your class that your best friend is angry with you.

What information do you need? _____

_____

Where can you get that information? _____

_____

You are having lots of nightmares every night.

What information do you need? _____

_____

Where can you get that information? _____

_____

Your grandparent is sick in the hospital.

What information do you need? _____

_____

Where can you get that information? _____

_____

Values and Goals

Look at the list of values words in Appendix E. Choose five of your most important values (things that are meaningful to you). Write these in the left column. Then, for each value, decide on a goal that matches it, what might be some barriers that would keep you from accomplishing your goal and, finally, what action steps you need to take in order to meet your goal.

Value	Goal	Barriers	Action steps to overcome barriers
Example: Education	Go to college	Bad grades Need help with homework	1. Ask teacher about tutoring 2. Do homework before playing

Goals, Goals, Goals

We can set goals in lots of different areas of our lives. For each of the different areas listed below, write down one of your goals.

Education _____

_____

Family _____

_____

Friends_____

_____

Behavior_____

_____

Body/Physical _____

_____

Fun _____

_____

CHAPTER 9

Competence, Mastery and Self-Efficacy

Introduction

A personal sense of competence, mastery and self-efficacy is critical to psychological health and well-being. In particular, a sense of competence and self-efficacy is an important determinant for how people behave and the choices they make. A sense of competence and self-efficacy enables a person to weather all types of negative life events and stressful situations (Conger and Conger 2002; Mirowsky and Ross 2003). However, self-efficacy has been found to be lower among adolescents of substance-abusing parents than among teens of non-substance-abusing parents (Mylant *et al.* 2002). These young people feel less pride in themselves and less satisfaction with their accomplishments.

Self-efficacy develops through multiple factors including perceptions of abilities, prior successes, amount of help received, perceived similarity to models, credibility of persuaders, and intensity of emotional/behavioral problems (Schunk 1995). For children of substance-abusing parents, many or all of these factors may be compromised.

Children need consistent emotional availability and nurturance from caregivers in order to develop internalized autonomy and confidence (Erikson 1950). Markowitz (2013) suggests that children of substance-abusing parents learn to numb their responses to positive experiences; that they feel safer remaining in a state of low self-esteem and moderate depression rather than taking the risk of feeling good about themselves.

Because children spend so much of their time in school, academic performance is an important factor in the development of mastery and competence. However, children of substance-abusing parents perform more poorly on academic measures than do children of non-substance-abusing parents (Johnson, Boney and Brown 1990; Sher 1997) and 41 percent of addicted parents reported that at least one of their children had repeated a grade (Kolar *et al.* 1994).

Best Practices and Treatment Recommendations

Research suggests that the key to effective intervention with children of substance abusers is encouragement of mastery (Werner and Johnson 2004). In fact, for most children, a sense of mastery or self-efficacy is an important factor in the development of self-esteem (Erol and Orth 2011).

Mastery experiences come in many forms, such as learning new skills, figuring out something, gaining insight, taking risks that pay off, etc. Werner and Johnson (2004) found that children of substance-abusing parents who grew into well-functioning adults developed a sense of competence and mastery by being involved in hobbies and activities that could distract them when things were going badly at home. Some of those activities included choir, orchestra, Scouts and church youth groups. Participation in organized activities, including afterschool activities, are associated with academic success, good mental health, satisfying social relationships and positive identity development (Mahoney, Larson and Eccles 2005). Wolin and Wolin (1996) describe initiative as a resiliency factor for children of addicted parents. They suggest that initiative offsets feelings of helplessness and can motivate engagement in hobbies and sports.

While not specifically investigated with children of substance-abusing parents, magic tricks are frequently used as an intervention technique to enhance mastery and self-esteem among children (Stenhouwer 1983). Using magic arts counseling, Levin (2007) found positive gains in self-esteem among children with behavioral problems; also using magic, Ezell and Klein-Ezell (2003) found significant increases in self-esteem and self-confidence among children with disabilities. While preliminary, researchers at the University of Hertfordshire compared students participating in a standard self-esteem lesson and students trained in performing magic, and found that the magic was more effective at promoting confidence and social skills (British Association for the Advancement of Science 2008). It may be that talents in magic elevate playground status and build a sense of competency.

Finally, a self-efficacy feature found to be a significant resiliency factor for children of alcoholics is taking on ability-appropriate, responsible roles (such as part-time paid work or caring for younger siblings). Researchers found that the children of alcoholics who grew into resilient adults often performed tasks that were helpful to others. They recommended "acts of required helpfulness" as a part of intervention programs, suggesting various types of community service (Werner and Johnson 2004).

General Suggestions

- Encourage children and their parents to participate in school- and community-based activities.

- Give children positive feedback regarding skills and competencies that you observe them performing (e.g. "You were very patient in waiting your turn," "That drawing really shows what a good eye you have for color").

- When teaching children new skills, emphasize the process rather than the outcome. Focus on the success of each step rather than simply the end result.

- Assist children in obtaining school success by finding tutors, intervening with teachers, etc.

- Don't do things for children that they can do for themselves.

- Encourage children to make friends with other children who believe in themselves and have high motivation for accomplishment. Self-efficacy is contagious!

- Highlight successes rather than failures.

- Remind children that competencies are often built on lots of mistakes and failures. Encourage them to try again because you believe in them.

- Introduce new experiences which will help children step outside of their comfort zones and expand their knowledge (trying new foods, going to new places, etc.).

Script

"Do you remember how you felt the last time you finished a project that you worked hard on? Or how you felt when you received a good grade on some schoolwork? I bet it felt great. Some of the feelings words that kids have used to describe how it felt to them are proud, pleased, excited, capable, smart, satisfied and inspired. It's certainly fabulous to feel those kinds of feelings!

Sometimes kids do things or accomplish things and don't give themselves credit for them. They think it's no big deal. But anytime you learn something new, take a risk or are successful doing something, it's an accomplishment and you should give yourself a pat on the back. That doesn't mean you have to brag about it but you can certainly let yourself feel proud of yourself.

What is something that you have done/accomplished that you didn't think you could do? Tell us about it."

Activities

(1) SUPER POWERS

OBJECTIVE
To identify an area of competence and mastery.

MATERIALS
A variety of printed Superhero base poses (Heromachine.com and Marvel.com allow you to create Superheroes online. However, for this activity, simply print out several base body types) and crayons or markers.

DIRECTIONS

Explain that all of us are really good at doing something even if we know other people who are better at it than we are. It's important not to compare ourselves to others but to look inside ourselves and acknowledge the things we do well. Then ask children to select one of the Superhero base poses that they feel represents the Superhero within them. Have them color it to represent their Superpower or strength (e.g. "Math Girl," "Builder Hercules," "Thoughtful Thor," etc.). Afterwards, ask children if they would like to share their Superhero with the group.

FOLLOW-UP DISCUSSION QUESTIONS

- If you could turn into your Superhero what kinds of things would you go around doing?

- What other things are you good at besides your Superhero's superpower?

- What things would you *like* to get good at and how would you do it?

- Do you have to be the best at something to feel good about it? Why?

(2) TALENT SHOW

OBJECTIVE

To find fun things to "show off" and build competence.

MATERIALS

Optional: some kind of "You've Got Talent" stickers or awards for participation.

DIRECTIONS

This activity requires preplanning. Be sure to inform the children ahead of time (one or two days) that you will be having a Talent Show. For those who would like to participate, they should consider dancing, singing, telling a joke, doing a magic trick, playing an instrument, making goofy faces, etc.

Explain to the group that everyone will take turns demonstrating their "talent" and that all talents will receive applause. Remind them to be supportive of one another and to have fun.

FOLLOW-UP DISCUSSION QUESTIONS

- Were you nervous getting up in front of the group? How did you overcome your nervousness?

- How did it feel to perform your talent? To receive applause?

- If we had another Talent Show, would you have something else that you could do?

- How many other people know that you have this talent?

(3) MY VALUES

OBJECTIVE

To identify and affirm personal values.

MATERIALS

Small or medium sized boxes with lids, watered-down glue or mod podge, cut-out values words (see Appendix E for values words)—make duplicates of ones that you think might be selected by more than one child), and various sizes and shapes and colors of cut-out construction paper.

DIRECTIONS

Explain that values are ideals that we believe are important. Each person has different values but all of us have them—even if we haven't thought about it before. Direct the children to look over the various cut-out values words and to select several that are significant/important to them. Have them decorate their boxes with values words and colorful paper pieces.

FOLLOW-UP DISCUSSION QUESTIONS

- What are some values that seem common among many of you?
- What are some unique values that each of you have?
- How do you stay true to your values?
- What kinds of things might you want to keep in your values box?

(4) PAPER BAG ME

OBJECTIVE

To acknowledge skills, abilities and character qualities.

MATERIALS

Small brown paper bags, lots of small slips of paper, pieces of fabric, glue, markers, crayons and colored pencils.

DIRECTIONS

Explain that people look one way on the outside and have parts of themselves that no one can see on the inside. Direct children to create a self-portrait on the outside of the paper bag. Then ask them to write down various skills, talents, abilities and character qualities on small pieces of paper and to put these inside the paper bag. Children may need prompts to think of as many things as possible to write on the pieces of paper. For example, you can ask what they have learned in school in order to have them identify that they can read, write, add, subtract, etc.

FOLLOW-UP DISCUSSION QUESTIONS

- What did you learn from this activity?

- Of the many things that you wrote on your pieces of paper, which are you proudest of?

- Looking at the many pieces of paper that you have in your bag, how do you feel about yourself?

- What kinds of new things would you like to learn?

(5) THE MAGIC TOUCH

OBJECTIVE

To learn a new skill and build a sense of competency.

MATERIALS

Aluminum pie plate, toothpicks and dish soap.

DIRECTIONS

Explain that doing magic tricks is a fun way to feel skilled and a good way to connect with other kids. Tell the children that you will teach them a magic trick that they can share with their friends and family.

Preparation for the magic trick (without the audience seeing): have children fill aluminum pie plates with just enough water to cover the bottom of the pie plates. Direct children to arrange four toothpicks in a square in the middle of their pie plates, making sure the ends of the toothpicks overlap. Have them dip a fifth toothpick in dish soap.

The trick: direct children to say a magic word or words, wave the toothpick dipped in dish detergent over the pie plate, and place the soap-dipped end into the middle of the square. The soap will cause the toothpicks to fly apart in the water. NOTE: There are many, many magic tricks that children can learn. Many of these can be found in books and on the internet. Don't limit yourself to just this one trick.

FOLLOW-UP DISCUSSION QUESTIONS

- Have you ever done a magic trick before? What was it?

- How did you like this magic trick?

- Who do you think you would like to perform this trick for? Who will you let in on the trick and teach her/him how to do it?

- How does it feel to know "magic?"

Worksheet Discussion Questions

What Can I Do? lists over 25 skills/competencies that many children can do. It simply asks children to circle the ones that they can do. After completing the worksheet, the following discussion questions can be used:

- How many things on the list are you able to do? What are they?
- How did you learn to do so many things?
- Were any of the things you circled difficult to learn? How did you keep yourself from giving up?
- What other things can you do that are not listed on this worksheet?

What Does It Say about Me? asks children to list some of the positive behaviors, activities or acts that they have done in the past and then asks them to go back over each one and to identify what each behavior says about them as people. The example that is given states, "I mopped the floors" and identifies "I'm a helpful person" from it. After completing the worksheet, the following discussion questions can be used:

- Did you realize that your activities and behaviors say something about you as a person?
- What did you learn about yourself from this worksheet?
- Are there other things that you could have listed on this worksheet? What are they?
- Looking over what you wrote, how do you feel about yourself?

"I Think I Can; I Think I Can" explains that giving up or being overly critical of oneself isn't healthy. It asks children to write encouraging things they can tell themselves when they feel discouraged or feel like giving up inside thought bubbles. After completing the worksheet, the following discussion questions can be used:

- Do you remember the story, *The Little Engine that Could?* What was the lesson he learned about what to say to himself?
- What are some of the negative thoughts you have to fight off when doing something that gets tough? What are some of the things you can tell yourself to keep from giving up or getting discouraged?
- Think of someone in your life who has accomplished a lot. What do you think she/he tells her/himself when things get tough?
- How important do you think it is to think positive thoughts? Why?

Ranking My Intelligences directs children to examine the eight different kinds of intelligences and to rank them in the order that they believe they possess each one (number 1 for highest; number 8 for lowest). It then asks them to consider what kinds of things they would be good at with the intelligences that they are strongest in. After completing the worksheet, the following discussion questions can be used:

- Did you realize that there were so many ways to be smart?

- What are your top three intelligences? Are you surprised to know this about yourself?

- What are some hobbies that you could develop with your kinds of intelligence? What kinds of jobs would you be good at with your kinds of intelligences?

- Do you know people who have similar types of intelligences as you? Are there things you could do together with these people?

Feeling Competent at School emphasizes the importance of school and asks children to evaluate themselves on ten factors that ensure school success. Afterwards it asks them about their strongest and weakest areas and a plan to correct the weak area. After completing the worksheet, the following discussion questions can be used:

- On a scale of 1–10 (with 1 being the lowest and 10 being the highest), how important is doing well in school to you? Why is it not a (*fill in a lower number*)?

- On a scale of 1–10 (with 1 being the lowest and 10 being the highest), how confident are you in your abilities to do well in school? Why is it not a (*fill in a lower number*)?

- When have you done well in school? How did that feel?

- How can you continue to do well in school?

What Can I Do?

Listed below are lots of competencies (abilities). Circle all the ones that you can do. You don't have to be great at them. You just have to know how to do them.

Collect things	Arrange flowers	Draw
Recycle	Play basketball	Dance
Run	Play baseball	Cook
Play soccer	Skate	Bake
Fly kites	Play an instrument	Sew
Camp	Shop	Cross stitch
Skateboard	Do crafts	Garden
Do crossword puzzles	Bowl	Swim
Hula-hoop	Laugh	Listen
Take pictures	Recognize stars	Read
Do puzzles	Plan activities	Play football
Play cards	Tell jokes	Pray
Write stories	Build models	Do yoga
Find things to do	Play volleyball	Start a DVD
Fix things	Meet new people	Save money
Solve riddles	Fix picnics	Type
Do math	Read a map	Help others
Take care of pets	Surf the internet	Mop
Ride a bicycle	Download apps	Exercise
Do homework	Babysit	Act in plays
Ride a horse	Play tennis	Sing
Fix my hair	Set the table	Knit
Pick out clothes	Explain things	Paint
Wash dishes	Dust	Organize
Make friends	Compliment others	Hike

Others? _____ _____ _____

What Does It Say about Me?

On the left side of the page, list some of the positive things you have done. These can be activities, accomplishments, acts of kindness, etc. After you have listed these, go back over each one and decide what this behavior says about you as a person. Write this on the right. An example is provided.

Thing I Did

Example: *I mopped the floors.*

What This Says about Me

I'm a helpful person.

"I Think I Can; I Think I Can"

Giving up or being too critical of yourself when learning something new isn't good for you. What are some positive things you can say to yourself if you are having trouble or if you don't think you did a good enough job? Write the positive thinking statements in the thought bubbles below. An example is given.

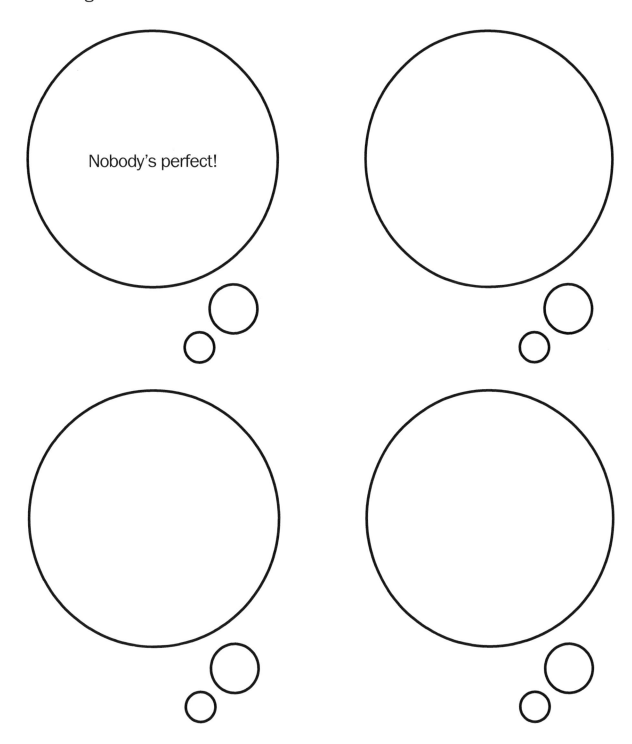

Nobody's perfect!

Ranking My Intelligences

Besides verbal and mathematic abilities, there are lots of other ways to be smart. Look at the different kinds of intelligences and their descriptions below. Then, on the lines to the left of each one, rank them in the order you think you possess them. Put number 1 by the one you think is your strongest, number 2 by the one you think is your second strongest, all the way to number 8.

_____ **Musical Intelligence:** You are sensitive to sounds, rhythms, pitch, meter, tones, melody and music.

_____ **Visual Intelligence:** You have a good sense of space and have the ability to see in your mind how things fit into spaces.

_____ **Verbal Intelligence:** You are good at reading, writing, telling stories and memorizing words.

_____ **Mathematical Intelligence:** You are good with numbers and reasoning.

_____ **Bodily or Kinesthetic Intelligence:** You are in control of your body's motions and are good at sports, dancing, acting and making things.

_____ **Interpersonal Intelligence:** You are sensitive to others' feelings and needs and can communicate effectively with others.

_____ **Intrapersonal Intelligence:** You enjoy figuring yourself out and have a deep understanding of your emotional self along with your strengths and weaknesses.

_____ **Naturalistic Intelligence:** You are sensitive to nature and have a good understanding of the world and your natural surroundings.

What is your number 1 intelligence? _____

What are some things you can do with that kind of intelligence? _____

_____

Feeling Competent at School

Doing well in school is important for life success and for feeling competent. Evaluate yourself on the following school success factors by marking an X under Always, Sometimes or Never. Then answer the questions at the bottom of the page.

Do I…	Always	Sometimes	Never
…get to school on time?			
…bring what I need to class?			
…do my classwork neatly?			
…pay attention in class?			
…turn in my homework?			
…study for tests?			
…do my best?			
…ask questions when I don't understand?			
…plan and organize my work?			
…realize the importance of school?			

Which area are you best at? _____

Which area do you need improvement on? _____

What is your improvement plan? _____

_____

Questions and Answers

QUESTION: What is addiction?

ANSWER: Addiction is a disease that makes someone crave drugs or alcohol. People who have the disease can't stop without help.

QUESTION: Can family members make a loved one stop drinking or using drugs?

ANSWER: No. An addict needs the help of people who are trained to treat the disease.

QUESTION: What are some of the physical symptoms of a hangover?

ANSWER: Nausea, fatigue, upset stomach, headache, sore muscles, "cotton mouth."

QUESTION: How does addiction start?

ANSWER: Doctors don't know the answer to that yet.

QUESTION: Why do people drink?

ANSWER: (any of these responses are correct) To unwind, to reward themselves, to fit in, to numb feelings, to feel less inhibited.

QUESTION: If someone who is addicted is sick why doesn't she/he just go to the doctor?

ANSWER: At first, the addict is not aware that she/he is ill. And part of the disease convinces people they don't have it.

QUESTION: What is a blackout?

ANSWER: When too much alcohol is in the body it can create a chemical disturbance in the brain, which makes it difficult to remember what happened while drinking—a bit like having temporary amnesia.

QUESTION: What is withdrawal?

ANSWER: When a person who has been drinking or using drugs too much suddenly stops, she/he can have physical symptoms for a while—kind of like getting sick.

QUESTION: What's the difference between a social drinker (SD) and a problem drinker (PD)?

ANSWER: (any of these responses are correct) SD knows when to stop/PD drinks to get drunk; SD never drives while drinking/PD does; SD drinks slowly and with food/PD gulps drinks; SD maintains her/himself while drinking/PD may become loud, angry, violent or silent.

QUESTION: Name one of the observable signs that someone is using marijuana.

ANSWER: (any of these responses are correct) Seems silly/giggly for no reason, has red/bloodshot eyes, seems dizzy and has trouble walking, has a hard time remembering things that just happened.

QUESTION: What is a 12-step program?

ANSWER: A support group that uses a set of 12 guiding principles which outline a plan for recovery from addiction.

QUESTION: What is alcohol tolerance?

ANSWER: Needing increasing amounts of alcohol to feel the same effects.

Coping Skills Bingo Cards

Bingo Card 1

Exercise	Listen to music	Write a letter	Relax	Think of a peaceful place
Count to 100	Say a tongue-twister five times	Sing	Play a musical instrument	Play a sport
Work in a garden	Talk to an adult	FREE	Talk to a friend	Clean something
Play with water	Take a bath	Think of puffy white clouds	Draw a picture	Blow bubbles
Dance	List things you are grateful for	Spend time with a pet	Play with clay	Make up a game

Bingo Card 2

Count to 100	Listen to music	Write a letter	Sing	Play with water
Work in a garden	Say a tongue-twister five times	Relax	Play a musical instrument	Play a sport
Think of a peaceful place	Blow bubbles	FREE	Talk to a friend	Clean something
Dance	Take a bath	Think of puffy white clouds	Draw a picture	Make up a game
Exercise	List things you are grateful for	Spend time with a pet	Play with clay	Talk to an adult

Bingo Card 3

Count to 100	List things you are grateful for	Write a letter	Talk to an adult	Take a bath
Work in a garden	Draw a picture	Make up a game	Play with water	Play a sport
Think of a peaceful place	Say a tongue-twister five times	FREE	Talk to a friend	Exercise
Dance	Blow bubbles	Think of puffy white clouds	Count to 100	Relax
Sing	Play a musical instrument	Clean something	Play with clay	Spend time with a pet

Bingo Card 4

Play with water	Count to 100	List things you are grateful for	Write a letter	Play a musical instrument
Work in a garden	Draw a picture	Make up a game	Talk to a friend	Talk to an adult
Think of a peaceful place	Say a tongue-twister five times	FREE	Exercise	Clean something
Dance	Blow bubbles	Think of puffy white clouds	Play with clay	Relax
Play a sport	Take a bath	Spend time with a pet	Sing	Listen to music

Bingo Card 5

Dance	Count to 100	List things you are grateful for	Talk to a friend	Blow bubbles
Work in a garden	Draw a picture	Make up a game	Listen to music	Play a sport
Say a tongue-twister five times	Think of a peaceful place	FREE	Play with clay	Clean something
Relax	Play with water	Play a musical instrument	Think of puffy white clouds	Sing
Talk to an adult	Take a bath	Spend time with a pet	Write a letter	Exercise

Bingo Card 6

Play with clay	Make up a game	List things you are grateful for	Talk to a friend	Talk to an adult
Draw a picture	Think of a peaceful place	Listen to music	Play a sport	Work in a garden
Say a tongue-twister five times	Dance	FREE	Exercise	Clean something
Relax	Take a bath	Blow bubbles	Think of puffy white clouds	Sing
Play a musical instrument	Count to 100	Spend time with a pet	Write a letter	Play with water

Impulses

1. You have the impulse to argue with your teacher.

2. You have the impulse to hit a classmate who made you angry.

3. You have the impulse to hide your family member's drugs or alcohol.

4. You have the impulse to borrow someone else's crayons without asking permission.

5. You have the impulse to break something when you're feeling angry.

6. You have the impulse to lie about your parent's drug or alcohol problem.

7. You have the impulse to interrupt a parent while she/he is talking.

8. You have the impulse to steal a piece of candy from your teacher's desk.

9. You have the impulse to yell at your parent when you thought she/he was being unfair to you.

10. You have the impulse to laugh at a classmate's new haircut.

11. You have the impulse to pet a strange dog.

12. You have the impulse to stay up late watching TV on a school night.

13. You have the impulse to drink some alcohol that your friend gives you.

14. You have the impulse to tear up a project because it's not perfect.

15. You have the impulse to sneak out of the house.

16. You have the impulse to hide everything under your bed instead of cleaning your room.

17. You have the impulse to insist on going first in a game.

18. You have the impulse to throw the game board when you lose.

19. You have the impulse to lie about brushing your teeth.

20. You have the impulse to push another kid who is in your way.

21. You have the impulse to cut in the lunch line in the cafeteria.

22. You have the impulse to lie about doing your homework.

23. You have the impulse to eat a whole bag of candy.

24. You have the impulse to run across the street.

25. You have the impulse to boss your brother or sister around.

Continuously Performed Behaviors

1. Clap your hands.
2. Stomp your feet.
3. Hum.
4. Nod your head "yes."
5. Shake your head "no."
6. Say "no" over and over.
7. Say "I won't" over and over.
8. Cry like a baby.
9. Make circles with your arms.
10. Rub your head.

Values Words

Honesty	Fun	Competition
Curiosity	Education	Beauty
Kindness	Wisdom	Open-mindedness
Faith	Compassion	Love
Friendship	Fairness	Accomplishment
Peace	Family	Trust
Humor	Loyalty	Responsibility
Freedom	Safety	Manners
Equality	Generosity	Strength
Tidiness	Organization	Creativity
Leadership	Happiness	Courage
Adventure	Belonging	Power
Spirituality	Curiosity	Gentleness
Nature	Physical strength	Service to others

APPENDIX F
Additional Activities

Chapters 1 or 6
I'D LIKE TO MEET SOMEONE

OBJECTIVE

To enhance group cohesion and establish new support systems.

MATERIALS

None.

DIRECTIONS

Direct the group to sit in a circle. Beginning with one child and moving around the circle several times (so that each child has several turns), have each child say on her/his turn, "I'd like to meet everyone who _____" (e.g. likes chocolate, is a Boy Scout, lives with only one parent, etc.). If any of the group members fit that description they should stand up and say, "Glad to meet you!" Continue for several rounds.

Chapters 2 or 3
TIME TO RELAX

OBJECTIVE

To decrease tension and increase relaxation.

MATERIALS

None.

DIRECTIONS

Explain to the group that bodies get tense when they are filled with worries and shame and that, in order to counter that tension, it can be helpful to do relaxation exercises. Instruct children to get comfortable in their seats or, if they prefer, they can lie on the floor. Ask them to follow your suggestions as you read a relaxation script in a calm, quiet voice. One is provided here:

> *Take a slow, deep breath…in with your nose and out with your mouth…and relax. Relax. Let your negative thoughts and worries drift away. Breathe slowly in…and out. Be aware of your breathing…and relax your body. Relax. (Longer pause.) Pay attention to your head. Make sure that it is relaxed. Let go of any tension. Continue breathing slowly in…and out…relax. Now pay attention to your neck…let relaxation melt into it…feel the warmth. Breathing slowly in…and out. Relax. (Longer pause.) Now focus on your shoulders…letting go of any tension that is trying to stay stuck there…breathing slowly in…and out…and relaxing…relaxing (Longer pause.) And pay attention to your chest. Feel it getting relaxed as you breathe slowly in…and out…slowly in…and out. And notice your hips as you feel that wonderful feeling of relaxation pour down into them…breathing slowly in…and out…in…and out. (Longer pause.) And gently begin to focus on your legs now…letting them enjoy that wonderful relaxation. Let them get comfortable and fully relaxed…breathing slowly in…and out. Relaxed. And, finally, pay attention to your feet and let them relax. Let your whole, entire body enjoy a completely relaxed state…as you slowly breathe in…and out…in…and out. (Longer pause.) And, as you feel ready, come back to our group with a relaxed body and calm mind.*

Chapter 4
INSIDE AND OUTSIDE FEELINGS

OBJECTIVE
To increase insight regarding hidden feelings.

MATERIALS
Paper plates, markers or crayons, a hole puncher and string.

DIRECTIONS
Explain to the group that people can sometimes feel one way on the outside and another way on the inside. You can also discuss the fact that children from substance-abusing homes often learn to hide some of their feelings. Then ask them to draw a feeling face on one side of the paper plate that shows the feeling that they let others see (their outside feeling) and, on the other side of the paper plate, ask them to draw a feeling face that shows the feeling that they keep hidden (their inside feeling). Then have them punch a hole on both sides of the paper plates and tie a piece of string in each hole, long enough so that they can tie the two pieces of string together to wear the paper plate as a mask.

MENU OF COPING SKILLS FOR ANGER

OBJECTIVE
To increase coping skills and decrease anger outbursts.

MATERIALS
Old restaurant menus, paper, glue and pens or markers.

DIRECTIONS
Remind the group how, when they go to a restaurant, they have many choices regarding what they can select to eat. In the same way, when they are feeling angry, they have many choices regarding what they can select to calm themselves. Then ask them to identify five to ten coping skills for anger and to write them on a piece of paper as different items on a "menu." Under each item, they can write a description of the coping skill much like a restaurant might do for a meal item. If they wish, they can also draw pictures of the coping skills much like a restaurant might have pictures of their entrees. After this is complete, have the children glue the paper to the inside of an old menu.

Chapter 5
ROLLING FOR SAFETY

OBJECTIVE
To identify safe and unsafe situations.

MATERIALS
One dice.

DIRECTIONS
Explain to the group that it is important for them to feel safe—to be in places where they feel safe and to be with people who make them feel safe. Have them sit in a circle and take turns rolling a dice. Using the topics below, ask the children to respond based on the number on the dice that they roll.

- Roll a one: talk about a time you did not feel safe at home.

- Roll a two: talk about a time you did not feel safe at school.

- Roll a three: name a person you feel safe with.

- Roll a four: name something that you do that keeps you safe.

- Roll a five: name a place where you feel safe.

- Roll a six: name something that makes drinking too much alcohol or taking mood-changing drugs unsafe.

Chapter 7

DANCING OPPOSITE

OBJECTIVE
To create a forced delay in order to think rather than simply act.

MATERIALS
Fast and slow music.

DIRECTIONS
Explain to the group that in this activity they will be dancing to music—except that instead of following their impulses to follow the rhythm of the music, you would like for them to dance fast to the slow music and dance slow to the fast music. Then play five to ten seconds of music before switching to another kind of music.

Chapter 9

YOU'VE GOT MAIL

OBJECTIVE
To increase self-esteem.

MATERIALS
Postcards, stamps and pens or pencils.

DIRECTIONS
Explain to the group that it is always fun to receive mail especially when it carries good news. Give each child a postcard and ask them to address it to themselves and then to write a note to themselves congratulating themselves for many of the skills and accomplishments that they have had so far in life. Collect the cards and mail them a week or two after the group.

NOTE: Supervise children's messages to themselves and do not allow any negative messages to be written.

MY FEEL GOOD FOLDER

OBJECTIVE
To create an object that can be used at home as a reminder of strength.

MATERIALS
Manila file folders, index cards, markers, glitter, decorative papers, stickers, glue and pens or pencils.

DIRECTIONS

Explain to the group that this project will be something they can use at home when they need to feel good about themselves. Explain that they will be creating a storage place for good feelings. Then have them write their names on the front of a folder followed by "Feel Good File" (e.g. "John's Feel Good File") and invite them to decorate their folders. Next, give each child enough index cards so that they can write a compliment to every other child in the group. When they are finished writing, have them hand the cards to the appropriate child. They will also be collecting cards from each other. After they have an opportunity to read the cards handed *to* them, instruct them to put the cards in their folders and, after they take the folders home, to continue putting things in them such as school awards, pictures of accomplishments, papers with good grades, etc.

Chapters 1–9

STINKIN' THINKIN' CHALLENGE

OBJECTIVE

To challenge negative cognitive distortions or irrational beliefs.

MATERIALS

Dry erase board or flip chart and markers.

DIRECTIONS

Have the group identify some of their negative thoughts. Write the thoughts on a dry erase board or flip chart one at a time. Then challenge the thoughts by using the following questions:

- Is this thought correct?
- What is the evidence that it is correct?
- Is there any evidence on the other side—that it is NOT correct?
- Does having this thought help me in any way? Does it hurt me in any way?
- What good things might happen if I let go of this thought?
- What's the worst thing that could happen if I let go of this thought?
- Am I willing to let go of this thought?
- How will I let go of it?

References

Ackerman, R.J. (1989) *Perfect Daughters*. Deerfield Beach, FL: Health Communications, Inc.

Adger, H. (2004) "The role of primary care physicians." Kensington, MD: National Association for Children of Alcoholics. Available at www.nacoa.net/role.htm, accessed on 29 December 2014.

Adult Children of Alcoholics World Service Organization (1978) "The Laundry List" (credited to Tony A.) Available at www.adultchildren.org/lit/Laundry_List.php, accessed on 29 December 2014.

American Academy of Experts in Traumatic Stress (2012) "Effects of parental substance abuse on children and families." Available at www.aaets.org/article230.htm, accessed on 29 December 2014.

Amodeo, M., Griggin, M.I.., Fassler, I., Clay, C. and Ellis, M.A. (2007) "Coping with stressful events: influence of parental alcoholism and race in a community sample of women." *Health and Social Work 32*, 2, 247–257.

Andrews, B. and Hunter, E. (1997) "Shame, early abuse, and course of depression in a clinical sample: a preliminary study." *Cognition and Emotion 11*, 373–381.

August, G.J., Realmuto, G.M., Hetkner, J.M., and Bloomquist, M.L. (2001) "An integrated components preventive intervention for aggressive elementary school children: the early risers program." *Journal of Consulting and Clinical Psychology 69*, 614–626.

Ayduk, O. and Kross, E. (2010) "Analyzing negative experiences without ruminating: the role of self-distancing in enabling adaptive self-reflection." *Social and Personality Psychology Compass 4*, 841–854.

Backett-Milburn, K., Wilson, S., Bancroft, A. and Cunningham-Burley, S. (2008) "Challenging childhoods: young people's accounts of 'getting by' in families with substance use problems." *Childhood 15*, 4, 461–479.

Ballard, M. and Cummings, E.M. (1990) "Response to adults' angry behavior in children of alcoholic and nonalcoholic parents." *The Journal of Genetic Psychology 151*, 2, 195–299.

Bancroft, A., Wilson, S., Cunningham-Burley, S., Backett-Milburn, K. and Masters, H. (2004) *Parental Drug and Alcohol Misuse: Resilience and Transition Among Young People*. Centre for Research on Families and Relationships, University of Edinburgh. York: Joseph Rowntree Foundation.

Bandura, A. (1982) "Self-efficacy mechanism in human agency." *American Psychologist 37*, 2, 122–147.

Barnard, M. and Barlow, J. (2003) "Discovering parental drug dependence: silence and disclosure." *Children and Society 17*, 1, 45–56.

Bays, J. (1992) "The care of alcohol- and drug-affected infants." *Pediatric Annals 21*, 8, 485–495.

Beardslee, W.R. and Podorefsky, D. (1988) "Resilient adolescents whose parents have serious affective and other psychiatric disorders: importance of self-understanding and relationships." *The American Journal of Psychiatry 145*, 1, 63–69.

Becker-Weidman, E.G., Jacobs, R.H., Reinecke, M.A., Silva, S.G., and March, J.S. (2010) "Social problem-solving among adolescents treated for depression." *Behaviour Research and Therapy 48*, 11–18.

Begun, A. and Zweben, A. (1990) "Assessment and treatment implications of adjustment and coping capacities in children living with alcoholic parents."*Alcohol Treatment Quarterly 7*, 23–40.

Bell, B. and Cohen, R. (1981) "The Bristol Social Adjustment Guide: comparison between the offspring of alcoholic and non-alcoholic mothers." *British Journal of Clinical Psychology 20*, 93–95.

Billick, S., Gotzis, A. and Burgert, W. (1999) "Screening for psychosocial dysfunction in the children of psychiatric patients." *Psychiatric Annals 29*, 8–13.

Billings, A.G., Kessler, M., Gomberg, C.A. and Weiner, S. (1979) "Marital conflict resolution of alcoholic and nonalcoholic couples during drinking and non-drinking sessions." *Journal of Studies on Alcohol 40*, 3, 183–195.

Black, C. (2010) *It Will Never Happen to Me: Growing Up with Addiction as Youngsters, Adolescents, Adults (Second Edition, Revised)*. Bainbridge Island, WA: MAC Publishing.

Brackett, M.A., Rivers, S., Reyes, M. and Salovey, P. (2012) "Enhancing academic performance and social and emotional competence with the RULER Feeling Words Curriculum." *Learning and Individual Differences 22*, 218–224.

Brisby, T., Baker, S. and Hedderwick, T. (1997) *Under the Influence: Coping with Parents Who Drink Too Much*. London: Alcohol Concern.

British Association for the Advancement of Science (2008) "Magic Can Conjure Up Confidence and Social Skills." *ScienceDaily*. Available at www.sciencedaily.com/releases/2008/09/080911142419.htm, accessed on 29 December 2014.

Brook, J. and McDonald, T. (2009) "The impact of parental substance abuse on the stability of family reunifications from foster care." *Children and Youth Services Review 31*, 2, 93–198.

Brooks, C. (1981) *The Secret Everyone Knows*. Center City, MN: Hazelden.

Burlingame, G.M., McClendon, D.T. and Alonso, J. (2011) "Cohesion in group therapy." *Psychotherapy 48*, 1, 34–42.

Carrica, J.L. (2009) "Humor styles and leadership styles: community college presidents." Dissertation, Wichita State University.

Christensen, E. (1997) "Aspects of a preventive approach to support children of alcoholics." *Child Abuse Review 6*, 24–34.

Christofferson, M. and Soothill, K. (2003) "The long-term consequences of parental alcohol abuse: a cohort study of children in Denmark." *Journal of Substance Abuse Treatment 25*, 107–116.

Cleaver, H., Unell, I. and Aldgate, J. (2011) *Children's Needs – Parenting Capacity: Child Abuse, Parental Mental Illness, Learning Disability, Substance Misuse, and Domestic Violence.* London: The Stationery Office.

Colonnesi, C., Draijer, E.M., Stams, G.J., Van der Bruggen, C., Bogels, S.M. and Noom, M.J. (2011) "The relation between insecure attachment and child anxiety: a meta-analytic review." *Journal of Clinical Child and Adolescent Psychology 40,* 4, 630–645.

Conger, R.D. and Conger, K.J. (2002) "Resilience in Midwestern families: selected findings from the first decade of a prospective, longitudinal study." *Journal of Marriage and Family 64,* 361–373.

Conner, N.W. and Fraser, M.W. (2011) "Preschool social-emotional skills training: a controlled pilot test of the Making Choices and Strong Families Programs." *Research on Social Work Practice 21,* 6, 699–711.

Cuijpers, P. (2005) "Prevention programmes for children of problem drinkers: a review." *Drugs: Education, Prevention and Policy 12,* 6, 465–475.

Day, C., Carey, M. and Surgenor, T. (2006) "Children's key concerns: piloting a qualitative approach to understanding their experience of mental health care." *Clinical Child Psychology and Psychiatry 11,* 1, 139–155.

Deblinger, E. and Runyon, M.K. (2005) "Understanding and treating feelings of shame in children who have experienced maltreatment." *Child Maltreatment 10,* 364–376.

Dies, R.R. and Burghardt, K. (1991) "Group interventions for children of alcoholics: prevention and treatment in the schools." *Journal of Adolescent Group Therapy 1,* 3, 219–234.

Dom, G., D'haene, P., Hulstijn, W. and Sabbe, B. (2006) "Impulsivity in abstinent early- and late-onset alcoholics: differences in self-report measures and a discounting task." *Addiction 101,* 50–59.

Eiden, R.D., Colder, C., Edwards, E.P. and Leonard, K.E. (2009) "A longitudinal study of social competence among children of alcoholic and nonalcoholic parents: role of parental psychopathology, parental warmth, and self-regulation." *Psychology of Addictive Behaviors 23,* 1, 36–46.

El-Guebaly, N. and Offord, D.R. (1977) "The offspring of alcoholics: a critical review." *American Journal of Psychiatry 134,* 357–366.

Elias, M.J. and Weissberg, R.P. (2000) "Primary prevention: educational approaches to enhance social and emotional learning." *Journal of School Health 70,* 5, 186–190.

Emshoff, J.G. and Price, A.W. (1999) "Prevention and intervention strategies with children of alcoholics." *Pediatrics 10,* 1112–1122.

Erikson, E.H. (1950) *Childhood and Society.* New York: Norton.

Erol, R.Y. and Orth, U. (2011) "Self-esteem development from age 14 to 30: a longitudinal study." *Journal of Personality and Social Psychology 101,* 3, 607–619.

Ezell, D. and Klein-Ezell, C.E. (2003) "M.A.G.I.C. W.O.R.K.S. (Motivating Activities Geared to Instilling Confidence – Wonderful Opportunities to Raise Kids' Self Esteem)." *Education and Training in Developmental Disabilities 38,* 4, 441–450.

Fals-Stewart, W., Kelley, M.L., Cook, C.G. and Golden, J.C. (2003) "Predictors of the psychosocial adjustment of children living in households of parents in which fathers abuse drugs: the effects of postnatal parental exposure." *Addictive Behaviors 28,* 1013–1031.

Fearon, R.P., Bakermans-Kranenburg, M.J., IJzendoorn, M.H., Lapsey, A.M. and Roisman, G.I. (2010) "The significance of insecure attachment and disorganization in the development of children's externalizing behavior: a meta-analytic study." *Child Development 81*, 2, 435–456.

Feiring, C., Taska, L. and Lewis, M. (1998) "The role of shame and attributional style in children's and adolescents' adaptation to sexual abuse." *Child Maltreatment 3*, 2, 129–142.

Felices, A. (2005) "Humor as an ingredient of the treatment in a therapeutic community for psychosis." *Therapeutic Communities 26*, 1, 19–32.

Felitti, V.J., Anda, R.F., Norenberg, D., Williamson, D.F. *et al.* (1998) "Relationship of childhood abuse and household dysfunction to many of the leading causes of death in adults. The Adverse Childhood Experiences (ACE) Study." *American Journal of Preventative Medicine 14*, 4, 245–258.

Fleischhaker, C., Böhme, R., Sixt, B., Brück, C., Schneider, C. and Schulz, E. (2011) "Dialectical Behavioral Therapy for Adolescents (DBT-A): a clinical trial for patients with suicidal and self-injurious behavior and borderline symptoms with a one-year follow-up." *Child and Adolescent Psychiatry and Mental Health 5*, 1, 3–12.

Flook, L., Smalley, S.L., Kitil, M.J., Galla, B.M. *et al.* (2010) "Effects of mindful awareness practices on executive functions in elementary school children." *Journal of Applied School Psychology 26*, 70–95.

Flores, P.J. (2001) "Addiction as an attachment disorder: implications for group therapy." *International Journal of Group Psychotherapy 51*, 63–81.

Fraser, M.W., Nash, J.K., Galinsky, M.J. and Darwin, K.M. (2000) *Making Choices: Social Problem Solving Skills for Children.* Washington, DC: National Association of Social Workers Press.

Gance-Cleveland, B. (2004) "Qualitative evaluation of a school-based support group for adolescents with an addicted parent." *Nursing Research 53*, 6, 379–386.

Gargallo, B. (1993) "Basic variables in reflection-impulsivity: a training programme to increase reflectivity." *European Journal of Psychology of Education 3*, 151–167.

Gilbert, P. (2009) *The Compassionate Mind.* London: Constable and Robinson.

Gilbert, P. and Procter, S. (2006) "Compassionate mind training for people with high shame and self-criticism: a pilot study of a group therapy approach." *Clinical Psychology and Psychotherapy 13*, 353–379.

Grant, B.F. (2000) "Estimates of US children exposed to alcohol abuse and dependence in the family." *American Journal of Public Health 90*, 112–115.

Greene, R.W., Ablon, J.S., Goring, J.C., Raezer-Blakely, L. *et al.* (2004) "Effectiveness of collaborative problem solving in affectively disregulated children with oppositional defiant disorder: initial findings." *Journal of Consulting and Clinical Psychology 72*, 6, 1157–1164.

Greene, R.W., Biederman, J., Zerwas, S., Monuteaux, M., Goring, J. and Faraone, S.V. (2002) "Psychiatric comorbidity, family dysfunction, and social impairment in referred youth with oppositional defiant disorder." *American Journal of Psychiatry 159*, 7, 1214–1224.

Gregg, M.E. and Toumbourou, J.W. (2003) "Sibling peer support group for young people with a sibling using drugs: a pilot study." *Journal of Psychoactive Drugs 35*, 3, 311–319.

Grella, C. and Greenwell, L. (2006) "Correlates of parental status and attitudes toward parenting among substance-abusing women offenders." *The Prison Journal 86*, 89–113.

Hadley, J.A., Holloway, E.L. and Mallinckrodt, B. (1993) "Common aspects of object relations and self-representations in offspring from disparate dysfunctional families." *Journal of Counseling Psychology 40*, 3, 348–356.

Hall, J.C. (2007) "An exploratory study of differences in self-esteem, kinship social support and coping responses among African American ACOAs and Non-ACOAs." *Journal of American College Health 56*, 1, 49–54.

Hansson, H., Rundberg, J., Zetterlind, U., Johnsson, K.O. and Berglund, M. (2006) "An intervention program for university students who have parents with alcohol problems: a randomized controlled trial." *Alcohol and Alcoholism 41*, 655–663.

Harbin, F. (2000) "Therapeutic work with children of substance misusing parents." In F. Harbin and M. Murphy (eds) *Substance Misuse and Child Care: How to Understand, Assist and Intervene when Drugs Affect Parenting.* Lyme Regis: Russell House Publishing.

Harter, S.L. (2000) "Psychosocial adjustment of adult children of alcoholics: a review of the recent empirical literature." *Clinical Psychology Review 20*, 311–337.

Hassan, K.E. and Mouganie, Z. (2014) "Implementation of the social decision-making skills curriculum on primary students (grades 1–3) in Lebanon." *School Psychology International 35*, 2, 167–175.

Haugland, B. (2003) "Paternal alcohol abuse: relationship between child adjustment, parental characteristics and family function." *Child Psychiatry and Human Development 34*, 2, 127–146.

Hayes, J., Gelso, C. and Hummel, A. (2011) "Managing countertransference." In J.C. Norcross (ed.) *Psychotherapy Relationships that Work (Second Edition).* New York: Oxford University Press.

Hayes, S.C., Luoma, J.B., Bond, F.W., Masuda, A. and Lillis, J. (2006) "Acceptance and commitment therapy: model, processes and outcomes." *Behavior Research and Therapy 44*, 1–25.

Heaney, C.A. and Israel, B.A. (2008) "Social networks and social support." In K. Glanz, B.K. Rimer and K.Viswanath (eds) *Health Behavior and Health Education: Theory, Research, and Practice.* San Francisco, CA: John Wiley and Sons.

Hogan, D. and Higgins, L. (2001) *When Parents Use Drugs: Key Findings from a Study of Children in the Care of Drug-using Parents.* Dublin: The Children's Research Centre.

Hook, A. and Andrews, B. (2005) "The relationship of non-disclosure in therapy to shame and depression." *British Journal of Clinical Psychology 44*, 425–438.

Howe, D., Brandon, M., Hinings, D. and Schofield, G. (1999) *Attachment Theory, Child Maltreatment and Family Support.* London: Macmillan.

Humke, C. and Schaefer, C.E. (1996) "Sense of humor and creativity." *Perceptual and Motor Skills 82*, 544–546.

Johnson, J., Boney, T. and Brown, B. (1990) "Evidence of depressive symptoms in children of substance abusers." *International Journal of the Addictions 25* (4-A), 465–479.

Kazdin, A.E., Siegel, T.C. and Bass, D. (1992) "Problem-solving skills training and parent management training in the treatment of antisocial behavior in children." *Journal of Consulting and Clinical Psychology 60*, 5, 733–747.

Kelley, M.L. and Fals-Stewart, W. (2004) "Psychiatric disorders of children living with drug-abusing, alcohol-abusing, and non-substance-abusing fathers." *Journal of the American Academy of Child and Adolescent Psychiatry 43*, 5, 621–628.

Kelley, M.L., Cash, T.F., Grant, A.R., Miles, D.L. and Santos, M.T. (2004) "Parental alcoholism: relationships to adult attachment in college women and men." *Addictive Behaviors 29*, 1633–1636.

Kenny, M.C., Capri, V.R., Thakkar-Kolar, R.R., Ryan, E.E. and Runyon, M.K. (2008) "Child sexual abuse: from prevention to self protection." *Child Abuse Review 17*, 36–54.

Klostermann, K., Chen, R., Kelley, M.L., Schroeder, V.M., Braitman, A.L. and Mignone, T. (2011) "Coping behavior and depressive symptoms in adult children of alcoholics." *Substance Use and Misuse 46*, 1162–1168.

Knop, J., Teasdale, T.W., Schulsinger, F. and Goodwin, D.W. (1985) "A prospective study of young men at high risk for alcoholism: school behavior and achievement." *Journal of Studies on Alcohol 46*, 4, 273–278.

Kolar, A.F., Brown, B.S., Haertzen, C.A. and Michaelson, B.S. (1994) "Children of substance abusers: the life experiences of opiate addicts in methadone maintenance." *American Journal of Drug and Alcohol Abuse 20*, 2, 159–171.

Kroll, B. (2004) "Living with an elephant: growing up with parental substance misuse." *Child and Family Social Work 9*, 129–140.

Kross, E. (2009) "When the self becomes other." *Annals of the New York Academy of Sciences 1167*, 35–40.

Lane, K.L., Gresham, F.M. and O'Shaughnessy, T.E. (2002) "Identifying, assessing, and intervening with children with or at risk for behavior disorders: a look to the future." In K.L. Lane, F.M. Gresham and T.E. O'Shaughnessy (eds) *Interventions for Children with or at Risk for Emotional and Behavioral Disorders*. Boston: Allyn and Bacon.

Lanius, R.A., Williamson, P.C., Densmore, M., Boksman, K. *et al.* (2004) "The nature of traumatic memories: a 4.0 tesla fMRI functional connectivity analysis." *American Journal of Psychiatry 161*, 1, 36–44.

Laybourn, A., Brown, J. and Hill, M. (1996) *Hurting on the Inside*. Aldershot: Avebury.

Levin, D. (2007) "Magic arts counseling: the tricks of illusion as intervention." *Georgia School Counselors Association Journal*, 14–23.

Lewis, M. (1992) *Shame: The Exposed Self*. New York: The Free Press.

Lieberman, D.Z. (2000) "Children of alcoholics: an update." *Current Opinion in Pediatrics 12*, 4, 336–340.

Lieberman, M.D., Eisenberger, N.I., Crockett, M.J., Tom, S.M., Pfeifer, J.H. and Way, B.M. (2007) "Putting feelings into words: affect labeling disrupts amygdala activity in response to affective stimuli." *Psychological Science 18*, 5, 421–428.

Locke, E.A. and Latham, G.P. (2002) "Building a practically useful theory of goal setting and task motivation." *American Psychologist 57*, 705–717.

Lukens, E.P. and McFarlane, W.R. (2004) "Psychoeducation as evidence based practice: considerations for practice, research and policy." *Brief Treatment and Crisis Intervention 4*, 3, 205–225.

Luoma, J.B., Kohlenberg, B.S., Hayes, S.C., Bunting, K. and Rye, A.K. (2008) "Reducing self-stigma in substance abuse through acceptance and commitment therapy: model, manual development, and pilot outcomes." *Addiction Research and Theory 16*, 2, 149–165.

Maag, J.W. (2006) "Social skills training for students with emotional and behavioral disorders: a review of reviews." *Behavior Disorders 32*, 1, 5–17.

Maggiore, R.P. (1983) "Helping the impulsive pupil use self-control techniques in the classroom." *Pointer 27*, 4, 38–40.

Mahoney, D.L., Burroughs, W.J. and Hieatt, A.C. (2001) "The effects of laughter on discomfort thresholds: does expectation become reality?" *The Journal of General Psychology 128*, 2, 217–226.

Mahoney, J.L., Larson, R.W. and Eccles, J. (2005) "Organized activities as contexts of development: extracurricular activities, after-school and community programs." Mahwah, NJ: Lawrence Erlbaum Associates.

Marco, J.H., Garcia-Palacios, A. and Botella, C. (2013) "Dialectical behavioral therapy for oppositional defiant disorder in adolescents: a case series." *Psicothema 25*, 2, 158–163.

Markowitz, R. (2013) "Dynamics and treatment issues with children of drug and alcohol abusers." In S.L.A. Straussner (ed.) *Clinical Work with Substance-Abusing Clients*. New York: Guilford Press.

Marks-Tarlow, T. (2012) "The play of psychotherapy." *American Journal of Play 4*, 3, 352–377.

Martin, R.A., Puhlik-Doris, P., Larsen, G., Gray, J. and Weir, K. (2003) "Individual differences in uses of humor and their relation to psychological well-being: development of the Humor Styles Questionnaire." *Journal of Research on Personality 37*, 48–75.

Mayer, J.D., Roberts, R.D. and Barsade, S.G. (2008) "Human abilities: emotional intelligence." *Annual Review of Psychology 59*, 507–536.

Mayhew, S. and Gilbert, P. (2008) "Compassionate mind training with people who hear malevolent voices: a case series report." *Clinical Psychology and Psychotherapy 15*, 113–138.

McDonell, M.G., Tarantino, J., Dubose, A.P., Matestic, P. *et al.* (2010) "A pilot evaluation of Dialectical Behavioral Therapy in adolescent long-term inpatient care." *Child and Adolescent Mental Health 15*, 4, 193–196.

Meftagh, S.D., Mohammadi, N., Ghanizadeh, A., Rahimi, C. and Najimi, A. (2011) "Comparison of the effectiveness of different treatment methods in children with attention deficit hyperactivity disorder." *Journal of Isfahan Medical School 29*, 148, 1–12.

Miranda, A., Presentacion, M.J., Siegenthaler, R. and Jara, P. (2011) "Effects of a psychosocial intervention on the executive functioning in children with ADHD." *Journal of Learning Disabilities 46*, 4, 363–376.

Mirowsky, J. and Ross, C.E. (2003) *Social Causes of Psychological Distress (Second Edition)*. New York: Aldine de Gruyter.

Mischel, W. and Ebbesen, E.B. (1970) "Attention in delay of gratification." *Journal of Personality and Social Psychology 16*, 2, 329–337.

Moe, J. (1993) *Discover…Finding the Buried Treasure*. Tucson, AZ: STEM Publications.

Moe, J., Johnson, J.L. and Wade, W. (2008) "Evaluation of the Betty Ford Children's Program." *Journal of Social Work Practice in the Addictions 8*, 4, 464–489.

Moe, J. and Pohlman, D. (1989) *Kids' Power: Healing Games for Children of Alcoholics*. Tucson, AZ: ImaginWorks.

Moeller, F.G. and Dougherty, D.M. (2002) "Impulsivity and substance abuse: what is the connection?" *Addiction Disorders and Their Treatment 1*, 3–10.

Moos, R.H. (1992) "Stress and coping theory and evaluation research: an integrated perspective." *Evaluation Review* 16, 534–553.

Moos, R.H. (2002) "The mystery of human context and coping: an unraveling of clues." *American Journal of Community Psychology 30,* 67–88.

Mylant, M., Ide, B., Cuevas, E. and Meehan, M. (2002) "Adolescent children of alcoholics: vulnerable or resilient?" *Journal of the American Psychiatric Nurses Association 8,* 2, 57–64.

Nastasi, B.K. and DeZolt, D.M. (1994) *School Interventions for Children of Alcoholics.* New York: Guilford Press.

National Association for Children of Alcoholics (2011) "Kit for Parents." Available at www. nacoa.org/pdfs/kit4parentsweb.pdf, accessed on 29 December 2014.

Newlin, C. (2011) *Overview of the Adverse Experiences in Childhood (ACE) Study.* National Children's Advocacy Center.

Parker, S. and Thomas, R. (2009) "Psychological differences in shame vs. guilt: implications for mental health counselors." *Journal of Mental Health Counseling 31,* 213–224.

Pasternak, A. and Schier, K. (2012) "The role reversal in the families of adult children of alcoholics." *Archives of Psychiatry and Psychotherapy 3,* 51–57.

Payton, J.W., Wardlaw, D.M., Graczyk, P.A., Bloodworth, M.R., Tompsett, C.J. and Weissberg, R.P. (2000) "Social and emotional learning: a framework for promoting mental health and reducing risk behaviors in children and youth." *Journal of School Health 70,* 5, 179–185.

Peterson, C., Park, N. and Seligman, M.E.P. (2006) "Greater strengths of character and recovery from illness." *Journal of Positive Psychology 1,* 17–26.

Potter-Efron, R. (2002) *Shame, Guilt and Alcoholism: Treatment Issues in Clinical Practice (Second Edition).* Binghamton, NY: The Haworth Press.

Poulou, M.S. (2014) "How are trait emotional intelligence and social skills related to emotional and behavioural difficulties in adolescents?" *Educational Psychology 34,* 3, 354–366.

Price, A.W. and Emshoff, J.G. (1997) "Breaking the cycle of addiction." *Alcohol Health and Research World 21,* 3, 241–246.

Price, A.W. and Emshoff, J.G. (2000) "Breaking the cycle of addiction: prevention and intervention with children of alcoholics." In S. Abbott (ed.) *Children of Alcoholics: Selected Readings (Vol. II).* Rockford, MD: National Association for Children of Alcoholics.

Quinn, A. and Shera, W. (2009) "Evidence-based practice in group work with incarcerated youth." *International Journal of Law and Psychiatry 32,* 5, 288–293.

Reinert, D.F. (1999) "Group intervention for children of recovering alcoholic parents." *Alcoholism Treatment Quarterly 17,* 4, 15–27.

Rivinus, T.M., Levoy, D., Matzko, M. and Seifer, R. (1992) "Hospitalized children of substance-abusing parents and sexually abused children: a comparison." *Journal of the American Academy of Child and Adolescent Psychiatry 31,* 6, 1019–1923.

Robinson, B.E. (1989) "Working with children of alcoholics." Lanham, MD: Lexington Books.

Robinson, J. (2010) *Don't Miss Your Life.* Hoboken, NJ: John Wiley and Sons, Inc.

Ruben, D.H. (2001) *Treating Adult Children of Alcoholics: A Behavioral Approach.* San Diego, CA: Academic Press.

Rubin, L. (1996) *The Transcendent Child: Tales of Triumph over the Past.* New York: Harper Perennial.

Ruiz-Aranda, D., Salguero, J.M., Cabello, R., Palomera, R. and Fernandez-Berrocal, P. (2012) "Can an emotional intelligence program improve adolescents' psychosocial adjustment? Results from the Intemo Project." *Social Behavior and Personality 40,* 8, 1373–1380.

Russell, M., Henderson, C. and Blume, S.B. (1984) *Children of Alcoholics: A Review of the Literature.* New York: Children of Alcoholics Foundation.

Schunk, D.H. (1985) "Participation in goal setting: effects on self-efficacy and skills of learning disabled children." *Journal of Special Education 19,* 307–317.

Schunk, D.H. (1990) "Goal setting and self-efficacy during self-regulated learning." *Educational Psychologist 25,* 71–86.

Schunk, D.H. (1995) "Self-efficacy and education and instruction." In J.E. Maddux (ed.) *Self-efficacy, Adaptation, and Adjustment: Theory, Research, and Applications.* New York: Plenum.

Shelton, D., Kesten, K., Zhang, W. and Trestman, R. (2011) "Impact of a Dialectic Behavior Therapy-Corrections Modified (DBT-CM) upon behaviorally challenged incarcerated male adolescents." *Journal of Child Adolescent Psychiatric Nursing 24,* 2, 105–113.

Sher, K.J. (1991) "Psychological characteristics of children of alcoholics: overview of research findings." *Recent Developments in Alcoholism: Vol. 9. Children of Alcoholics.* New York: Plenum Press.

Sher, K.J. (1997) "Psychological characteristics of children of alcoholics." *Alcohol Health and Research World 21,* 3, 247–254.

Sher, K. and Trull, T. (1994) "Personality and disinhibitory psychopathology: alcoholism and antisocial personality disorder." *Journal of Abnormal Psychology 103,* 92–102.

Sher, K.J., Walitzer, K.S., Wood, P.K. and Brent, E.E. (1991) "Characteristics of children of alcoholics: putative risk factors, substance use and abuse, and psychopathology." *Journal of Abnormal Psychology 4,* 427–448.

Shirk, S. and Karver, M. (2003) "Prediction of treatment outcome from relationship variables in child and adolescent therapy: a meta-analytic review." *Journal of Consulting and Clinical Psychology 71,* 462–471.

Siu, A.M.H. and Shek, D.T.L. (2010) "Social problem solving as a predictor of well-being in adolescents and young adults." *Social Indicators Research 95,* 3, 393–406.

Smith, M. and Walden, T. (1999) "Understanding feelings and coping with emotional situations: a comparison of maltreated and nonmaltreated preschoolers." *Social Development 8,* 1, 93–116.

Sprecher, S. and Regan, P. (2002) "Liking some things (in some people) more than others: partner preferences in romantic relationships and friendships." *Journal of Social and Personal Relationships 19,* 463–481.

Stein, J.A., Rotheram-Borus, M.J. and Lester, P. (2007) "Impact of parentification on long-term outcomes among children of parents with HIV/AIDS." *Family Process 46,* 317–333.

Stein, N., Folkman, S., Trabasso, T. and Richards, T.A. (1997) "Appraisal and goal processes as predictors of well-being in bereaved caregivers." *Journal of Personality and Social Psychology 72,* 872–884.

Stenhouwer, R.C. (1983) "Using magic to establish rapport and improve motivation in psychotherapy with children: theory, issues, and technique." *Psychotherapy in Private Practice 1*, 2, 85–94.

Stoltenberg, S.F., Hill, E.M., Mudd, S.A., Blow, F.C. and Zucker, R.A. (1999) "Birth cohort differences in features of antisocial alcoholism among men and women." *Alcoholism: Clinical and Experimental Research 23*, 12, 1884–1891.

Takahashi, M. and Inoue, T. (2009) "The effects of humor on memory for nonsensical pictures." *Acta Psychologica 132*, 1, 80–84.

Tan, S.A., Tan, L.G., Lukman, S.T. and Berk, L. (2008) "Humor-associated mirthful laughter, as an adjunct therapy in cardiac rehabilitation, attenuates catecholamines and myocardial infarction recurrence." *Advanced Mind Body Medicine 22*, 3, 8–12.

Tangney, J.P. and Dearing, R.L. (2002) *Shame and Guilt.* New York: Guilford Press.

Tarter, R.E., Kirisci, L., Mezzich, A., Cornelius, J.R. *et al.* (2003) "Neurobehavioral disinhibition in childhood predicts early age at onset of substance use disorder." *American Journal of Psychiatry 160*, 1078–1085.

Tarter, R.E., Kirisci, L., Habeych, M., Reynolds, M. and Vanyukov, M. (2004) "Neurobehavior disinhibition in childhood predisposes to substance use disorder by young adulthood: direct and mediated etiologic pathway." *Drug and Alcohol Dependence 73,* 121–132.

Tracy, E. and Martin, T. (2007) "Children's roles in the social networks of women in substance abuse treatment." *Journal of Substance Abuse Treatment 32*, 81–88.

Tullett, A.M. and Inzlicht, M. (2010) "The voice of self-control: blocking the voice increases impulsive responding." *Acta Psychologica 135*, 252–256.

Ulutas, I. and Omeroglu, E. (2007) "The effects of an emotional intelligence education program on the emotional intelligence of children." *Social Behavior and Personality 35*, 10, 1365–1372.

US Department of Health and Human Services, Administration for Children and Families (2002) *Substance Abuse and Child Maltreatment.* National Clearinghouse on Child Abuse and Neglect and Information.

US Department of Transportation, National Highway Traffic Safety Administration (NHTSA) *Traffic Safety Facts 2012: Alcohol-Impaired Driving.* Washington, DC. Available at www-nrd.nhtsa.dot.gov/Pubs/811870.pdf, accessed on 29 December 2014.

Velleman, R. and Orford, J. (1999) *Risk and Resilience: Adults Who Were the Children of Problem Drinkers.* Amsterdam: Harwood Academic Publishers.

Werner, E.E. (1986) "Resilient offspring of alcoholics: a longitudinal study from birth to age 18." *Journal of Studies on Alcohol 47*, 1, 34–40.

Werner, E.E. and Johnson, J.L. (2004) "The role of caring adults in the lives of children of alcoholics." *Substance Use and Misuse 39*, 5, 699–720.

Werner, E.E. and Smith, R. (1989) *Vulnerable but Invincible: A Longitudinal Study of Resilient Children and Youth.* New York: Adams, Bannister and Cox.

Werner, E.E. and Smith, R.S. (1992) *Overcoming the Odds: High Risk Children from Birth to Adulthood.* Ithaca, NY: Cornell University Press.

Wiechelt, S.A. (2007) "The specter of shame in substance misuse." *Substance Use and Misuse 42*, 399–409.

Wolin, S. and Wolin, S.J. (1996) "The challenge model: working with strengths in children of substance-abusing parents." *Adolescent Substance Abuse and Dual Disorders 5*, 1, 243–257.

Wolin, S.J. and Wolin, S. (1993) *The Resilient Self: How Survivors of Troubled Families Overcome Adversity.* New York: Villard Books.

Zylowska, L., Ackerman, D.L., Yang, M.H., Futrell, J.L. *et al.* (2008) "Mindfulness mediation training in adults and adolescents with ADHD: a feasibility study." *Journal of Attention Disorder 11*, 6, 737–746.

Subject Index

Author Index